MASTERING GRC

The Lawyer's Guide to Success in Governance, Risk, and Compliance

CAROLE STERN SWITZER

AMERICAN BAR ASSOCIATION
Solo, Small Firm and
General Practice Division

Cover design by Mary Anne Kulchawik/ABA Design

Library of Congress Cataloging-in-Publication Data

Names: Switzer, Carole Stern, 1956- author
Title: Mastering GRC : the lawyer's guide to success in governance, risk, and compliance / Carole Stern Switzer.
Description: Chicago : American Bar Association, 2025. | Includes index. | Summary: "In today's rapidly evolving business landscape, the role of lawyers in an integrated approach to governance, risk management, and compliance (GRC) has become increasingly important. Mastering GRC: The Lawyer's Guide to Success in Governance, Risk, and Compliance is a comprehensive resource designed to equip legal professionals with the knowledge, tools, and strategies necessary to navigate this multifaceted field. As organizations face mounting regulatory pressures, heightened stakeholder expectations, and an ever-changing risk landscape, lawyers find themselves at the forefront of efforts to ensure organizational integrity, resilience, and success. The information and guidance provided in this book are designed to assist lawyers in meeting the challenge, whether they work in-house in a large corporation or a small/medium enterprise (SME), government agency, or law firm. The book references "your client organization," which may mean the company or division you serve as an in-house team member, your client if you are situated in a law firm or advisory firm, or the government agency in which you are employed"-- Provided by publisher.
Identifiers: LCCN 2025020463 | ISBN 9781639056439 paperback | ISBN 9781639056446 epub
Subjects: LCSH: Lawyers--United States | Practice of law--United States | Lawyers--Vocational guidance--United States | Corporate governance--Law and legislation--United States | Risk management--Law and legislation--United States | Compliance auditing--United States
Classification: LCC KF300 .S95 2025 | DDC 340.023/73--dc23/eng/20250418
LC record available at https://lccn.loc.gov/2025020463

Printed in the United States of America.

29 28 27 26 25 5 4 3 2 1

ISBN 978–1-63905-643-9

Contents

About the Author .... **vii**
Executive Summary .... **ix**

Introduction **1**
Why This Book Is Needed 1
Who This Book Is For 9
How to Use This Book 10

1 Integrating Legal Expertise into GRC **13**
Introduction 13
Balancing Legal Considerations with Business Objectives 14
Aligning Legal Strategy with GRC Objectives 18
Cross-functional Collaboration in GRC: The Lawyer as Leader 21
Legal's Role in Risk Management 26
Navigating GRC in Highly Regulated Industries 28
Cross-Border Integration of Legal Expertise in GRC 32
Conclusion 34
Action Items 34
Interview with Son-U Michael Paik **35**

2 Core GRC Roles for Lawyers **39**
Introduction 39
Evaluating the Operational Context of the Business 39
Designing an Aligned Business Plan 49

Operationalizing GRC Strategies 59
Improving GRC Capabilities 74
Conclusion 81
Action Items 82
Interview with Judit Seymour 82

3 Ethical Considerations in GRC 87
Introduction 87
The Evolving Ethical Landscape 88
Building an Ethical GRC Culture 93
Ethics in the International Business Context 95
Conclusion 98
Action Items 99
Interview with Joe Murphy 99

4 The Role of Lawyers in GRC Stakeholder Management 105
Introduction 105
The Lawyer's Unique Position in Stakeholder Management 106
The Importance of Understanding GRC Capabilities 107
Strategies for Managing Various Stakeholders 108
Challenges and Considerations 110
Conclusion 110
Action Items 111
Interview with Bettye Hill 111

5 The Role of Lawyers in Crisis Management 115
Introduction 115
Understanding the Landscape 115
The Lawyer's Role in Crisis Preparedness 116
Navigating the Storm: Legal Considerations in Crisis Response 117
Business Continuity: Ensuring Organizational Resilience 117
Learning from the Crisis: Post-Event Considerations 118

Ethical Considerations: Navigating the Gray Areas ... 119
Leveraging Technology in Crisis Management ... 119
Conclusion ... 120
Action Items ... 120
Interview with Tom Fox ... 121

6 Using GRC Technology ... 123
Introduction ... 123
Overview of GRC Technology Landscape ... 123
The Future of GRC Technologies ... 124
International Variations and Challenges in GRC Technology Use ... 129
Challenges and Considerations ... 133
Strategies for Effective Technology Adoption ... 134
Conclusion ... 135
Action Items ... 135

7 Challenges and Opportunities ... 137
Introduction ... 137
Navigating Dual Roles: Legal Advisor and Business Partner ... 138
Lawyers' Strengths and Weaknesses ... 141
Managing Resource Constraints and Priorities ... 144
Effective Communication of Legal Risks ... 148
Continuous Improvement in Legal GRC Processes ... 152
Conclusion ... 156
Action Items ... 156
Interview with Jonathan Strassberg ... 157

8 Future Trends in GRC and the Evolving Role of Lawyers ... 161
Introduction ... 161
Technological Revolution in GRC ... 162
The Shifting Regulatory Landscape ... 163
Evolving Corporate Governance Models ... 165

The Evolving Role of Lawyers 165
Conclusion 166
Action Items 166
Interview with Scott Mitchell 167

9 Building a GRC-Focused Legal Career 173
Introduction 173
Private Sector Career Paths in GRC for Lawyers 173
Government Roles in GRC 176
International Roles for Lawyers in GRC 177
Key Skills to Develop 180
Education and Certifications 181
Career Advancement Strategies 185
Conclusion 186
Action Items 187

Index **189**

About the Author

Carole Stern Switzer, Esq., is the cofounder of the global nonprofit think tank OCEG, joining founder Scott L. Mitchell in January 2003. The organization's initial mission was to improve corporate compliance and ethics by developing standards, and so it was called the Open Compliance and Ethics Group. As that work began in the spring of 2003, conversations amongst the drafting committee members expanded beyond compliance and ethics—moving into performance management, risk management, governance, and assurance. The team decided that what was needed were standards for a fully integrated approach to all these organizational aspects, focusing primarily on governance, risk management, and compliance. So OCEG created the term *GRC* to represent these (and additional) capabilities that would ensure the integration of governance, assurance, and management of performance, risk, compliance, and ethics.

Over the past 20+ years, Carole has been a leading expert in GRC, writing frequently on the topic and presenting keynote addresses at numerous events globally. She has continued to define and refine GRC concepts, authoring numerous resources published by OCEG and providing articles for many magazines and other publications.

Prior to cofounding OCEG, Carole had a 20-year legal career, during which she was a partner in the Washington, DC, offices of several national law firms, where she had a widely recognized environmental law practice. She represented corporate clients primarily regarding issues arising under the Resource, Conservation, and Recovery Act (RCRA) and the Comprehensive Environmental Compensation and Liability Act (CERCLA), more commonly known as the Superfund law.

During this time, she was an active member of the ABA, serving on the Council of the (now named) Environment, Energy, and Resources

Section and chairing the Solid and Hazardous Waste Committee. She was appointed to a three-year term on the ABA Standing Committee on Environmental Law. She also was recognized in the Martindale-Hubbell Bar Register of Preeminent Women Lawyers.

Carole's legal practice included litigation regarding the application of environmental regulations before the DC Circuit and the US Supreme Court, representation of Superfund defendants, legislative analysis and drafting, and counseling regarding all environmental compliance and risk aspects. She assisted clients in designing and implementing environmental compliance programs and performed assessments of such programs. This experience informed her work as a primary author of OCEG's first GRC Capability Model.

Executive Summary

In today's rapidly evolving business landscape, the role of lawyers in an integrated approach to governance, risk management, and compliance (GRC) has become increasingly important. ***Mastering GRC: The Lawyer's Guide to Success in Governance, Risk, and Compliance*** is a comprehensive resource designed to equip legal professionals with the knowledge, tools, and strategies necessary to navigate this multifaceted field. As organizations face mounting regulatory pressures, heightened stakeholder expectations, and an ever-changing risk landscape, lawyers find themselves at the forefront of efforts to ensure organizational integrity, resilience, and success. The information and guidance provided in this book are designed to assist lawyers in meeting the challenge, whether they work in-house in a large corporation or a small/medium enterprise (SME), government agency, or law firm. The book references "your client organization," which may mean the company or division you serve as an in-house team member, your client if you are situated in a law firm or advisory firm, or the government agency in which you are employed.

Introduction to GRC for Lawyers

The concept of GRC has undergone a significant transformation over the past two decades. What was once a set of siloed functions has evolved into an integrated, strategic approach essential for organizational success. This evolution reflects the growing recognition that governance, risk management, and compliance are interconnected aspects of organizational management that, when properly aligned, can drive performance and create value.

This shift presents both challenges and opportunities. The traditional role of legal professionals as technical experts in law has expanded dramatically. Today's lawyers are expected to be strategic partners in GRC efforts, contributing not just legal expertise but also business acumen and strategic insight. This book aims to bridge the gap between legal knowledge and the broader world of GRC, providing readers with the tools they need to excel in this expanded role.

The Evolving Role of Lawyers in GRC

The transformation of the lawyer's role in GRC is one of the central themes of this book. Modern organizations expect their legal professionals to go beyond traditional legal advisory functions. Today's lawyers in GRC roles are called upon to contribute meaningfully to strategic decision-making processes, bringing legal perspective to business strategy. You should proactively manage many risks that impact business objectives, not just legal compliance. By doing so, you can help drive value creation through innovative legal and compliance activities. Alignment of legal strategies with overall business goals ensures that legal considerations support rather than hinder business objectives. When your governance team sees this, it will invite you to participate in strategic planning and review.

This expanded role requires lawyers to wear multiple hats, balancing their responsibilities as legal advisors with their new role as business partners. The chapters that follow explore in depth how to effectively navigate this dual role, addressing common challenges such as maintaining objectivity in business decisions, developing the necessary business acumen, and managing the constraints that come with broader responsibilities.

Key Components of GRC for Lawyers

To excel in GRC, you must comprehensively understand its key components and how they intersect with legal expertise. This book provides in-depth coverage of these core aspects:

Understanding the Operational Context

Lawyers play a pivotal role in analyzing the external and internal factors shaping an organization's GRC landscape. This involves a multifaceted approach that is not limited to reviewing internal policies and procedures to ensure full coverage of legal requirements. It also includes conducting thorough assessments of legal, regulatory, and political factors across various jurisdictions and analyzing compliance culture and ethical standards within the client organization. In addition, lawyers play a key part in managing relationships with key stakeholders, including regulatory bodies and government agencies. By developing expertise in these areas, you can provide invaluable insights that inform GRC strategies and decision-making processes.

Designing an Aligned Business Plan

Legal professionals are instrumental in ensuring that a client organization's business plan aligns with GRC principles. They help set ambitious and legally sound organizational direction and objectives while identifying opportunities, obstacles, and obligations from a legal and compliance perspective. In this role, you will evaluate and refine approaches to risk, reward, and compliance by operationalizing GRC strategies through the development of processes for policy development, effective communication, and comprehensive training programs. This involvement ensures that legal and ethical considerations are woven into the client organization's strategic planning from the outset.

Operationalizing GRC Strategies

Lawyers play a vital role in translating GRC strategies into practical, day-to-day operations. As a legal professional, you may contribute to the implementation of GRC initiatives across the client organization in many ways, including:

- **Establishing Actions and Controls:** Lawyers help develop a mix of proactive, detective, and responsive controls to address opportunities, obstacles, and obligations. They ensure these controls are legally sound, effective, and aligned with the organization's risk tolerance.
- **Policy Management:** Legal experts often lead or heavily contribute to policy development and lifecycle management. They craft clear, enforceable policies that address legal and compliance requirements while supporting business objectives.

- **Communication and Reporting:** Lawyers ensure that the right information reaches the right audiences at the right time. They contribute to developing stakeholder reports, internal communications, and regulatory filings, balancing transparency with the protection of sensitive information.
- **Education and Training:** Legal professionals participate in the development of education and support programs. They create content for legal and compliance training, conduct workshops, and help ensure that employees understand their GRC responsibilities.
- **Incentivizing Desired Conduct:** Lawyers advise on structuring incentive programs that encourage ethical behavior and compliance without perverse incentives or legal risks.
- **Managing Issue Notification and Response:** Legal experts help design and implement systems for reporting and addressing both favorable and unfavorable events, ensuring these systems meet legal requirements and protect the organization's interests.

By actively engaging in these operational aspects of GRC, you help ensure that legal and compliance considerations are effectively integrated into your client organization's daily activities and decision-making processes.

Improving GRC Capabilities

Continuous improvement is a hallmark of effective GRC, and lawyers play a key role in driving this process. Your responsibilities may include monitoring the effectiveness and efficiency of GRC actions and controls, providing assurance about priority areas in GRC to stakeholders, identifying areas for improvement, and implementing beneficial changes to GRC processes.

Participating actively in these activities can help ensure that your client organizations' GRC capabilities evolve to meet new challenges and opportunities.

Integrating Legal Expertise Across the GRC Framework

One of the most valuable contributions you can make to GRC is the integration of legal expertise across the entire framework applied in your client organization. Strategies for achieving this integration include supporting the development and maintenance of robust governance structures and positioning legal advice as an enabler of strategic initiatives rather than a roadblock. When you are viewed as a member of the strategic team, you can develop approaches to legal efforts that align with the organization's overall risk appetite and implement proactive compliance strategies that anticipate and mitigate potential issues.

Your role in these strategic approaches will develop further as you demonstrate the value these efforts bring to the achievement of objectives.

Ethical Considerations in GRC

Ethical considerations are at the heart of effective GRC, and lawyers are often at the forefront of addressing these issues. The unique ethical challenges lawyers face in GRC roles include balancing the need for confidentiality with demands for transparency, managing potential conflicts of interest in dual advisory and business partner roles, addressing the ethical implications of new technologies in GRC practices, and navigating cross-border ethical considerations in global organizations.

You can have a key role in establishing guidance for ethical decision-making and strategies for building and maintaining an ethical GRC culture within your client organization.

Challenges and Strategies for Lawyers in GRC

The expanded role of lawyers in GRC comes with significant challenges. It addresses key issues such as managing resource constraints and competing priorities in GRC activities, effectively communicating legal risks to diverse stakeholders across the organization, and driving continuous improvement in legal GRC processes in the face of organizational inertia.

As discussed in Chapter 7, there are practical, actionable strategies for each of these challenges that you can implement in your daily practice. You can also leverage your unique strengths as a lawyer and address common weaknesses to enhance your effectiveness in GRC roles.

Technology and the Future of GRC

As technology continues to reshape the business landscape, it's also transforming GRC practices. The use of technology is no longer an option; it is a necessity. You must understand the technological trends that are shaping the future of GRC and how you can leverage these tools to enhance your effectiveness. Key areas of focus include:

- The application of artificial intelligence and machine learning in GRC processes
- The potential of blockchain and distributed ledger technology for enhancing transparency and trust
- The use of advanced data analytics and visualization tools for risk management and compliance monitoring
- Emerging trends such as robotic process automation and the Internet of Things and their implications for GRC

Chapters 6 and 8 explore the opportunities presented by these technologies and address the challenges they pose, including ethical considerations and the need for ongoing learning and adaptation among legal professionals.

Building a GRC-Focused Legal Career

Chapter 9 of this book serves as a comprehensive road map for lawyers looking to build or advance their careers in GRC. It outlines career paths in both the private and public sectors, detailing the responsibilities and progression opportunities. The chapter also provides insights into the key skills you must develop to excel in GRC roles, including legal competencies and essential business skills.

Additionally, the chapter covers relevant certifications and educational opportunities to enhance your GRC credentials. It also offers networking and professional development strategies, emphasizing the importance of building a strong professional network in this rapidly evolving field.

Conclusion: The Lawyer as GRC Leader

As GRC continues to evolve and increase in importance, lawyers have a unique opportunity to position themselves as indispensable strategic partners in their client organizations' success. By embracing the multifaceted role of the GRC leader, lawyers can drive the integration of legal considerations into broader GRC frameworks and help organizations navigate regulatory landscapes. By leading cross-functional collaboration in GRC initiatives and championing ethical practices, they can grow success for both their client organizations and their own careers.

Mastering GRC: The Lawyer's Guide to Success in Governance, Risk, and Compliance provides a comprehensive road map for legal professionals to enhance their effectiveness in GRC roles, add strategic value to their organizations, and advance their careers in this growing and evolving field. Whether working in large corporations, small/medium enterprises (SMEs), law firms, or government entities, lawyers equipped with the insights and strategies from this book are well-positioned to lead their client organizations toward sustainable success in a challenging business and regulatory environment.

Introduction

Why This Book Is Needed

GRC Is Maturing and Driving Success for Many Organizations

GRC, the acronym that represents integrated governance, risk management, and compliance, was originated as a business concept by the Open Compliance and Ethics Group (now referred to as OCEG) in 2002–2003. It represents the intertwined collection of capabilities that enable an organization to achieve Principled Performance, which OCEG defines as the ability to reliably achieve objectives, address uncertainty, and act with integrity.[1] More than 20 years later, GRC is widely understood and used worldwide by businesses and governments. This has led to the creation of a multibillion-dollar legal, advisory, and technology market of services and tools specifically designed to help businesses, governments, and other types of organizations mature their GRC capabilities. OCEG's GRC Capability Model is the authoritative standard practice framework that supports these efforts.[2] The GRC Glossary is the definitive source of definitions for terms that are regularly applied in GRC contexts. It should be consulted if the reader does not understand any terms used in this book.[3]

---

[1] OCEG defines and addresses GRC and Principled Performance. Principled Performance is a registered trademark of OCEG and is used in this guide with permission from OCEG.

[2] The GRC Capability Model is a free and open-source framework including core GRC standards available at https://www.oceg.org/grc-standards/#grc-capability-model.

[3] The GRC Glossary can be found at https://www.oceg.org/glossary/.

GRC is an integrated operating framework that aligns an organization's strategies, processes, technology, and people to effectively manage risks, meet regulatory requirements, and, most fundamentally, achieve established objectives. As organizations face continuously changing regulations and stakeholder expectations, governance, risk management, compliance, and other relevant areas of operation have evolved from siloed functions into a cohesive, organization-wide approach to decision-making and operational excellence.

GRC has matured significantly in recent years, transforming from a reactive, compliance-driven necessity to a proactive organizational success driver. This maturation is characterized by:

- **Integration:** Breaking down silos between governance, risk management, compliance, and other related functions to create a unified, holistic approach and use of data
- **Strategic Alignment:** Embedding GRC principles and practices into core business processes and decision-making to support organizational objectives at every level
- **Technology Adoption:** Leveraging advanced analytics, artificial intelligence, and automation to enhance risk detection, monitoring, and reporting capabilities
- **Embedded Culture:** Fostering a culture of risk awareness and ethical behavior throughout the organization, from the board level to frontline employees
- **Continuous Improvement:** Implementing robust feedback mechanisms and adaptive processes to ensure the GRC framework evolves with changing business and regulatory landscapes

Organizations that have successfully implemented mature GRC frameworks are reaping significant benefits, including:

- Enhanced decision-making through improved risk visibility and data-driven insights
- Increased efficiency and reduced costs through streamlined processes and automation
- Stronger resilience to disruptive events and market volatility
- Improved stakeholder trust and brand reputation

- More effective resource allocation and prioritization of risk mitigation efforts
- Better positioning to capitalize on strategic opportunities while managing risks

As GRC has continued to evolve, it has become an integral part of organizational strategy and a key differentiator in today's competitive business landscape. Both in-house and outside lawyers must help to bridge the gap between legal requirements, business objectives, and risk management strategies. Consequently, your need to understand the relationships between the establishment of business objectives and strategies, risk management decision-making, and compliance with legal requirements has never been greater.

This book provides legal professionals with the knowledge needed to navigate the intricate world of GRC. It enables you to add significant value to your client organization and enhance your career in an era when the effective integration of governance, risk management, and compliance is more critical than ever.

While GRC principles apply to large corporations and governmental entities, they are equally important for small and medium-size enterprises (SMEs), which face unique challenges in implementing GRC frameworks due to limited resources and smaller organizational structures. GRC leaders must scale their approach appropriately for SMEs, focusing on key risks and regulatory requirements without creating unnecessary bureaucracy. As a lawyer advising organizations of any size, you must be adept at developing pragmatic, cost-effective GRC solutions that provide essential protections without overburdening the business.

A note about who you serve: Throughout the book, there are references to "your client organization," which may mean your corporate client if you are situated in a law or advisory firm, the company or division you serve as an in-house team member, or the government agency in which you are employed. In other words, not only lawyers in law firms have clients. If you work within a legal department, take a direct role in a compliance or risk management department, or serve in a governance capacity, you must remember that the organization you serve is your client. You are responsible for supporting its objectives by aligning legal strategies with the client's business goals to facilitate successful outcomes.

Lawyers Are Protectors

Many writers address the various roles that contribute to GRC, but OCEG offers the clearest concept: It calls GRC professionals "Protectors" who simultaneously produce and preserve value for their clients. This description should resonate with you. As Protectors, lawyers are at the forefront of addressing the tremendous value destruction caused by unprincipled misconduct, mistakes, and miscalculations. To tackle these challenges, they work with other GRC professionals in governance, strategy, risk, compliance, security, and audit roles. The legal perspective is the thread that weaves through and connects these various disciplines, ensuring a cohesive and legally sound approach to GRC.

Lawyers embody the dual nature of Protectors described by OCEG. They simultaneously play offense and defense, dispelling the misconception that their role is purely defensive. Lawyers are quintessential two-way players in the corporate world. They produce value by facilitating strategic transactions, identifying growth opportunities, and crafting innovative legal solutions. At the same time, they preserve value by mitigating risks, ensuring compliance, and safeguarding the organization's interests in an ever-shifting regulatory landscape.

The mountain-climbing analogy used by OCEG in its discussion about Protectors resonates strongly with the legal profession.[4] As organizations climb toward their objectives, lawyers act as both the ropes and the clamps, securing progress and preventing fatal missteps. They draft contracts that lock in value, develop compliance programs that act as safety harnesses, and provide legal insights and analysis that help navigate treacherous regulatory terrain. In doing so, they prevent value-destroying falls into legal and regulatory crevasses.

Importantly, lawyers integrate seamlessly with the GRC-critical disciplines that OCEG defines.[5] In governance and oversight, they advise

[4] https://www.oceg.org/ideas/what-is-a-protector/.

[5] https://www.oceg.org/ideas/critical-disciplines/.

boards and executives on legal and ethical responsibilities. In strategy and performance, they provide legal frameworks for strategic initiatives. In risk and decision-making, they assess legal risks and guide informed choices. In compliance and ethics, they design and implement robust programs. In security and continuity, they address legal aspects of data protection and business resilience. In audit and assurance, they support legal compliance audits and investigations. An in-house lawyer may serve not only within a legal department but also directly in any of the critical discipline roles.

A Common Pitfall to Avoid

The tendency toward tunnel vision can significantly diminish effectiveness as lawyers strive to be Protectors. Those in outside counsel positions and some in-house counsel may inadvertently narrow their focus to purely legal considerations, overlooking the broader business context in which their advice applies.

This myopic approach can lead to suboptimal organizational outcomes. While legal compliance is undoubtedly crucial, it should not exist in a vacuum. Virtually all legal work for a client organization necessitates a comprehensive understanding and consideration of the organization's objectives and strategies, whether at the highest organizational level or the department or project level relevant to the matter at hand. This broader perspective serves two purposes.

First, it ensures that your legal advice or approach does not unnecessarily impede established objectives or strategies. While there may be instances when difficulty achieving legal compliance or a high risk of noncompliance requires a change in business direction, such situations should be clearly communicated to the client, allowing for informed decision-making. Understanding the operating context allows you to craft solutions that achieve legal compliance while minimizing disruption to the organization's goals.

Second, and equally important, this holistic understanding enables you to effectively articulate how your work supports and advances the client's objectives and strategies. By demonstrating this alignment, you can enhance your value proposition and strengthen your role as a trusted advisor to the organization. This ability to speak the language of business and show tangible contributions to organizational goals is what truly elevates a lawyer from a mere legal technician to an indispensable Protector in the GRC framework.

To truly embody the Protector role, you must see yourself as an integral part of the business, not adjacent to it. This means actively understanding the organization's market position, competitive landscape, strategic goals, and operational challenges. It involves regular communication with business leaders, participation in strategic planning sessions, and a willingness to engage with non-legal aspects of the business. By doing so, you can provide more nuanced, context-aware advice that protects the organization from legal risks and actively contributes to its success and growth.

Corporate Lawyers Fill Key Roles in GRC, Whether They Know It or Not

Lawyers serving corporate clients have traditionally been categorized based on their primary area of practice, with three main categories emerging as the most common: litigators, transactional lawyers, and regulatory lawyers. Litigators are known for their work in dispute resolution, representing clients in court proceedings, arbitrations, and other forms of conflict management. Transactional lawyers, on the other hand, focus on facilitating business plans, drafting and negotiating contracts, and structuring corporate deals. This category includes corporate lawyers specializing in mergers and acquisitions, tax, and real estate.

Regulatory lawyers form the third major category, encompassing a broad range of specialists who navigate multiple and sometimes contradictory regulations. This group includes lawyers focusing on specific industries or areas of law, such as environmental regulations, data privacy, anti-corruption, international trade, taxation, intellectual property, and employment law.

In addition to these three main groups, lobbyists form a distinct category of professionals. Many of them have law degrees and use their legal expertise to influence legislation, regulations, and government policies on behalf of their clients. It is worth noting that many regulatory lawyers also engage in lobbying within their specialized fields, demonstrating the overlapping nature of these categories.

While useful for understanding the broad landscape of legal practice, these categories are not mutually exclusive. Many lawyers, particularly those working in-house for corporations or large law firms, may operate across multiple categories as they address their clients' or employers' diverse legal needs. This flexibility and breadth of expertise become particularly relevant in the context of GRC, where you need to draw on skills and knowledge from various practice areas to navigate organizational challenges effectively.

While deeply involved in activities integral to GRC, many lawyers do not explicitly recognize their work as part of this broader framework. This lack of recognition can stem from the traditional categorization of legal roles and the tendency to view legal work as separate from other business functions. However, the reality is that corporate lawyers, both in-house and outside, play a crucial role in enabling their client organization to achieve Principled Performance—the ability to reliably achieve objectives, address uncertainty, and act with integrity.[6]

Corporate lawyers contribute to Principled Performance in numerous ways without labeling their activities as GRC related. For instance, lawyers inherently manage risk when drafting and negotiating contracts and ensure compliance with applicable laws and regulations. They directly contribute to the *G* in GRC by structuring deals, performing merger and acquisition due diligence, and advising on corporate governance matters. Their role in identifying and mitigating legal risks, whether in transactions, operations, or litigation, is a key aspect of the *R* in GRC. Their work in interpreting regulations, advising on compliance matters, and helping implement internal policies and procedures is central to the *C* in GRC.

Moreover, corporate lawyers may serve as their organizations' ethical compass, promoting integrity in business practices and decision-making. This aligns directly with the "act with integrity" aspect of Principled Performance. Their advisory role in strategic planning and major business decisions helps organizations address uncertainty and achieve their objectives, further contributing to Principled Performance.

The integrated nature of GRC capabilities is particularly evident in the work of corporate lawyers. For example, when a lawyer advises on a new business initiative, they are not just providing legal advice in isolation. They consider governance structures, assess risks, ensure

[6] https://www.oceg.org/ideas/what-is-principled-performance/.

compliance with relevant laws and regulations, and help implement controls—all of which are interconnected aspects of GRC.

Recognizing your work as an integral part of GRC can more effectively align your activities with broader organizational goals and strategies. This leads to more proactive engagement in GRC initiatives, better collaboration with other functions such as risk management and compliance, and a more robust and integrated approach to achieving Principled Performance. It also positions you as a key strategic partner in your client organization's efforts to meet its objectives while maintaining ethical standards and complying with regulatory requirements.

Lawyers in the Public Sector Have GRC Roles and Influence the GRC Landscape

Public sector entities have different primary objectives than businesses but face equally difficult governance, risk, and compliance challenges. As a public sector lawyer, you must be adept in adapting GRC principles to the unique needs of public sector organizations. This requires navigating the intersection of public policy, regulatory compliance, and operational efficiency to implement robust risk management practices within budgetary and political constraints. By collaborating across departments and agencies to create an integrated GRC framework, you can address the unique ethical considerations in government GRC practices. This will contribute to enhancing transparency and accountability in government operations, balancing public interest considerations with effective governance.

Whether working in a department general counsel's office, serving on a specialized agency or legislative committee legal team, or advising government entities as outside counsel, as a public sector lawyer, you can leverage GRC principles to enhance governance, mitigate risks, and ensure compliance with the web of laws and regulations governing public entities. You can play a crucial role in ensuring that government agencies comply with applicable laws and regulations and manage legal risks associated with public policy decisions, government operations, and interactions with the private sector.

In addition, as a government lawyer in a legislative, regulatory, or enforcement role, you may directly influence the GRC landscape for all organizations by drafting legislation, creating regulations, and enforcing them both. You can help set the standards corporate lawyers must interpret and apply. Simply put, government lawyers are the architects of the compliance frameworks that corporate lawyers must navigate.

Moreover, government lawyers engaged in regulatory enforcement, whether in a government agency or an enforcement branch of a justice department, are key stakeholders in many organizations' GRC efforts. By recognizing the role of government lawyers in the broader GRC ecosystem, we can better appreciate the full scope of legal involvement in GRC processes, from the creation of regulatory frameworks to their implementation and enforcement in both the public and private sectors.

Who This Book Is For

This book is intended to be a resource for a wide range of legal professionals who interact with organizational clients or aspire to do so. Specifically, it is designed for:

- **Corporate and In-House Counsel:** Lawyers working directly within organizations need to understand their role in the broader GRC framework and effectively integrate legal considerations with business objectives.
- **Outside Counsel and Law Firm Attorneys:** Practitioners who advise organizational clients will gain insights into providing more holistic, business-aligned legal advice beyond mere compliance to add strategic value.
- **Lawyers Across Various Sectors:** Whether you serve businesses, educational institutions, nonprofit organizations, government entities, or other organizations, this book offers applicable principles and strategies for enhancing your GRC-related work.
- **Lawyers in Government Regulatory Agencies and Legislative Committees:** Attorneys involved in drafting, implementing, or enforcing laws and regulations will gain insights into creating more effective, risk-aware, and compliance-friendly regulatory frameworks that align with broader GRC principles.
- **Public Sector Lawyers:** Those responsible for adapting GRC principles to the unique needs of public sector organizations.
- **Legal Professionals in Specialized Fields:** Whether your focus is compliance, risk management, corporate governance, or any other

area intersecting with GRC, this book offers valuable insights for enhancing your specialized practice.

- **Experienced Lawyers Seeking Growth:** Seasoned attorneys looking to expand their practice areas or increase their influence with clients will find new perspectives and approaches to elevate their advisory capabilities.
- **Aspiring GRC Professionals:** The book is an excellent primer for lawyers considering a transition into dedicated GRC roles. It explains how legal skills can be leveraged in this multidisciplinary field.
- **Non-Lawyer Executives and Board Members:** While primarily aimed at legal professionals, this book can also benefit organizational leaders seeking to better understand and collaborate with their legal teams on GRC matters.
- **Recent Law School Graduates:** The book provides a comprehensive understanding of GRC principles for those starting their legal careers, helping shape a career path that aligns with the evolving needs of organizational clients.
- **Legal Educators and Students:** The book is a practical supplement to academic coursework for law professors and students interested in corporate law, compliance, and risk management.

The book equips you, as a legal professional at any career stage, to enhance your value to clients by providing a comprehensive overview of GRC principles, a discussion of the core practices, and insights into lawyers' evolving role in this space. It bridges the gap between legal expertise and business acumen, enabling you to position yourself as an indispensable advisor in the ever-evolving GRC landscape.

Whether you are looking to start your career on a strong footing, pivot your existing practice, or stay ahead of the curve in an ever-changing legal and business environment, ***Mastering GRC: The Lawyer's Guide to Success in Governance, Risk, and Compliance*** provides the knowledge and tools you need to succeed.

How to Use This Book

This book is designed to be a comprehensive resource for legal professionals at various stages of their GRC journey. The book often refers to *you* when describing different GRC roles and responsibilities that lawyers undertake. Of course, you won't be filling every role or taking on all the responsibilities for lawyers in GRC, but you will identify areas of responsibility that you currently have or that you may strive to fulfill. To get the most out of this book, consider the following approach:

- **Start with the Basics:** If you are new to GRC, read straight through from the start to gain a solid foundation of core concepts, understand why GRC is crucial for modern organizations, and understand how lawyers fit in.
- **Assess Your Current Role:** Identify which GRC roles or responsibilities you currently fulfill and which you might aspire to in the future.
- **Dive Deep into Relevant Chapters:** While reading the entire book is recommended, you may want to prioritize chapters most relevant to your current challenges or career goals.
- **Reflect on Scenario Examples:** Many chapters include example situations. Take time to consider how these scenarios might apply to you or your client organization.
- **Implement Action Items:** At the end of each chapter that follows, you will find action items. Consider how you can apply these in serving your client organization.
- **Revisit and Review:** GRC is an evolving field. Periodically revisit chapters to refresh your knowledge and gain new insights as your experience grows.
- **Share and Discuss:** Consider discussing the concepts with colleagues. GRC is inherently collaborative, and sharing perspectives can enhance understanding.
- **Plan Your GRC Career:** Map out your GRC career path and identify areas for professional development, including certifications.

This book is not just a one-time read but a resource to consult throughout your GRC journey. Whether you are facing a specific challenge or looking to expand your role, you will find relevant insights and practical advice within these pages.

Chapter 1
Integrating Legal Expertise into GRC

Introduction

Lawyers bring a unique set of skills and knowledge that can significantly enhance GRC program effectiveness. Your analytical nature, honed through years of interpreting laws and regulations, allows you to understand and assess multifaceted GRC issues. Translating the language of legislation and regulatory requirements so they can be put into actionable business practices enables better governance at every level of the business.

As your expertise is applied throughout the GRC lifecycle, you must strike a balance between legal considerations and business objectives. This balance is at the heart of effective GRC integration, requiring lawyers to be not just legal advisors but strategic partners in the organization's success.

As a lawyer, you possess a distinctive perspective on risk assessment that stems from your training in identifying potential legal pitfalls and their consequences. This foresight, combined with expertise in reasoning and decision-making, enables you to contribute meaningfully to risk management structures and policy development. Your contract-analysis and dispute-resolution skills further bolster an organization's ability to manage relationships and mitigate risks.

Perhaps most critically, you can bring an in-depth understanding of the ever-evolving regulatory landscape to your client organization. This knowledge allows you to anticipate changes, adapt strategies proactively, and ensure that GRC programs remain robust and current. This is particularly important for highly regulated industries and where cross-border operations arise. By integrating these legal insights throughout the GRC lifecycle, organizations can create more resilient, compliant, and ethically sound operational frameworks based on an invaluable perspective about potential threats and mitigation strategies.

Balancing Legal Considerations with Business Objectives

One of the most challenging aspects of integrating legal expertise into the GRC framework is striking the right balance between legal considerations and business objectives. This balancing act is at the heart of effective in-house legal counsel and is also increasingly important for outside counsel. You must navigate this delicate balance to ensure legal compliance without unnecessarily hindering business growth and innovation.

Understanding Business Strategy

The foundation of this balancing act is a deep understanding of the organization's business objectives and strategy. You cannot effectively balance legal considerations with business objectives if you do not fully grasp them and how the organization plans to achieve them. This goes beyond a surface-level understanding of an organization's products or services; it requires a nuanced comprehension of the organization's goals and strategic plans, competitive landscape, and market dynamics.

To achieve this, you should actively engage with business leaders deeply and often. This might involve participating in strategic planning sessions, attending business unit meetings, or simply having regular conversations with executives and managers. The goal is to understand what the business is doing, why it is doing it, and where it aims to go.

For example, lawyers who understand that their company is pursuing an aggressive growth strategy in emerging markets are better equipped to provide legal advice that supports this objective while managing the associated risks. They might focus on developing flexible contract templates that can be easily adapted to different jurisdictions or on creating compliance training programs that address the specific challenges of operating in new markets.

Risk-Informed Decision-Making

With a solid understanding of business strategy in place, you can provide risk-based legal advice that considers business implications. This involves more than simply identifying legal risks; it requires weighing those risks against potential business benefits and helping business leaders make informed decisions.

For instance, when presented with a new business opportunity that carries some legal risk, you should not simply advise against it. Instead, you should help business leaders understand the nature and extent of the legal risks, the potential consequences, and mitigation strategies. You might present several options, each with different risk profiles, allowing the business leaders to make an informed decision based on their risk appetite and strategic priorities.

This approach requires thinking beyond black-and-white legal analysis. You need to consider the broader business context, including competitive pressures, market opportunities, and potential financial impacts. By providing this contextualized advice, you can help ensure that legal considerations are properly balanced against business objectives.

Enabling Compliant Innovation

In today's fast-paced business world, innovation is key to success. However, innovative ideas can sometimes push the boundaries of existing legal and regulatory frameworks. Lawyers can contribute to enabling compliant innovation.

This involves working proactively with R&D and product development teams, not as gatekeepers but as enablers. You should strive to identify legal pathways for innovative ideas and find ways to achieve business objectives within the bounds of the law. This might involve creative yet defensible interpretations of existing regulations, engaging with regulators to seek guidance or exceptions, or developing new compliance frameworks that allow for flexibility and innovation.

For example, a lawyer working with a financial technology (fintech) company might help develop a new financial product that pushes the boundaries of existing regulations. Rather than simply rejecting the idea, they might work with the product team to design features that achieve the business objective while remaining compliant, and they might engage with regulators to seek approval for this innovative approach.

Communicating Effectively

Effective communication is key to balancing legal considerations with business objectives. You must be able to translate legal concepts into business-friendly language and clearly articulate the business case for legal recommendations.

This involves more than just simplifying legal jargon. It requires framing legal advice in terms of business impact and opportunities. For instance, rather than just warning about the legal risks of a proposed action, you might present it in terms of how it could affect market share, customer relationships, or long-term growth prospects.

Developing strong relationships with business leaders is key to fostering open dialogue. You should strive to be approachable and collaborative, encouraging business teams to involve you early in the decision-making process. This allows legal considerations to be integrated seamlessly into business planning rather than being seen as a last-minute obstacle. For in-house counsel, the goal is to develop a relationship that lets business leaders view the legal department as the "department of know" rather than the "department of no."

Quantifying Legal Risk

One powerful way to balance legal considerations with business objectives is to quantify legal risks and the value of legal risk management. This involves collaborating with finance and other departments to put numbers to potential legal risks and costs.

For example, you might work with the finance team to calculate the potential costs of a regulatory violation, including fines, legal fees, and lost business. They could then compare this to the cost of implementing stronger compliance measures. This quantitative approach can help business leaders understand the ROI of compliance and make more informed decisions about resource allocation.

You should also develop metrics that demonstrate the value of legal risk management. This might include tracking the number of disputes avoided through proactive legal intervention or measuring the financial impact of favorable contract negotiations.

Continuous Improvement

Balancing legal considerations with business objectives is not a static task. It requires continuous improvement and adaptation. You should regularly review and update your legal team strategies to ensure they remain aligned with evolving business objectives and legal landscapes.

This involves seeking feedback from business units on the effectiveness of legal support. Are legal teams seen as enablers or obstacles? Are legal processes helping or hindering business operations? This feedback can inform improvements in legal services and processes.

It is also important to stay informed about industry trends and best practices in legal risk management. You should continuously educate yourself about new legal technologies, innovative compliance strategies, and evolving business models in your client organization's industry.

Ethical Leadership

Lawyers take part in ethical leadership by balancing legal considerations with business objectives. You should advocate for ethical business practices that align with long-term organizational success, helping cultivate a culture where legal and ethical considerations are viewed as business enablers rather than obstacles.

This involves more than just ensuring technical compliance with laws and regulations. It requires promoting a broader understanding of the value of ethical business practices. You can help business leaders understand how strong ethics and compliance can enhance brand reputation, build customer trust, and create long-term sustainable value.

For instance, you might advocate for adopting stringent data protection practices that go beyond mere legal compliance. While this may seem like an added burden in the short term, you should articulate how it can become a competitive advantage, differentiating the company in a market increasingly concerned about data privacy.

Bringing Value

By effectively balancing legal considerations with business objectives, you can position yourself as a valuable strategic partner who contributes directly to the organization's success. This balanced approach ensures robust governance, effective risk management, and steadfast compliance while supporting innovation and growth. It transforms the legal function from a cost center to a value creator, integral to the organization's strategic success.

Aligning Legal Strategy with GRC Objectives

Integrating legal expertise into the broader GRC framework begins by aligning legal strategy with the overarching GRC objectives. This alignment ensures that legal efforts protect the organization and actively contribute to its strategic goals and operational efficiency.

Understanding the GRC Landscape

Before alignment can occur, you must comprehensively understand the organization's GRC landscape by familiarizing yourself with the current state of governance structures, risk management, and compliance programs. You need to identify key stakeholders in each of these aspects of the GRC process. You also need to identify and understand the organization's risk appetite and tolerance levels, outline its strategic objectives, and identify how GRC supports these goals.

Mapping Legal Touchpoints

Understanding the GRC landscape requires careful analysis of how legal considerations intersect with and weave through each aspect of governance, risk, and compliance. Corporate governance structures carry significant legal implications, from board member fiduciary duties to shareholder rights and reporting requirements. Intellectual property protection must be strategically aligned with business objectives through proper legal frameworks, including patents, trademarks, and trade secrets that safeguard competitive advantages.

The legal dimension of GRC extends deeply into regulatory compliance across jurisdictions, where lawyers must navigate complex and sometimes conflicting requirements while ensuring consistent global operations. Contract management sits at the intersection of legal oversight and operational risk, requiring attorneys to balance business flexibility with risk mitigation through carefully structured agreements while maintaining awareness of how contract terms impact everything from supply chain resilience to data protection obligations.

You should develop a full understanding of these legal touchpoints as they are specifically designed in your organization and identify areas where there may be gaps or overlaps requiring some reconsideration.

Developing an Integrated Legal Strategy

With a clear understanding of the GRC landscape and legal touchpoints, you can develop a legal strategy that aligns with and supports GRC objectives by establishing:

- **A Risk-Based Approach:** Prioritize legal efforts based on the organization's risk profile and tolerance levels. This ensures that legal resources are allocated efficiently and in line with GRC priorities.
- **Proactive Compliance:** Move beyond reactive legal problem-solving to proactive compliance strategies that anticipate and mitigate risks before they materialize.
- **Governance Support:** Develop legal frameworks that enhance corporate governance structures, ensuring they are robust, compliant, and aligned with best practices.
- **Strategic Enablement:** Position legal advice and services as enablers of strategic initiatives rather than obstacles by finding creative, compliant solutions to business challenges.

Collaborative Integration

Alignment requires close collaboration between GRC functions, which will be enhanced by having regular meetings with risk management and compliance teams to discuss emerging legal risks. Members of the legal team should partner with compliance officers to develop effective compliance programs. Work with internal audit to ensure legal considerations are addressed in audit processes, and engage with business units to understand objectives so they can provide tailored legal support.

The more you engage with and come to know the individuals on these teams, the more likely they are to actively involve you at the start of projects rather than waiting until problems arise.

Performance Metrics and Measurement

Key performance indicators (KPIs) are used throughout businesses to provide quantifiable measurements indicating progress toward strategic objectives and early warning signals when course corrections are needed. KPIs help transform abstract goals into concrete metrics that can be tracked, analyzed, and acted upon. They enable organizations to make data-driven decisions while creating accountability at all levels through clear, measurable targets.

Too often, legal departments do not effectively utilize KPIs, even though they can serve multiple crucial purposes, such as demonstrating the department's value contribution to the broader organization, highlighting areas requiring additional resources or attention, and providing evidence of control effectiveness for auditors and regulators. These metrics can track everything from contract turnaround times and regulatory finding resolution rates to more sophisticated measurements like risk reduction percentages or compliance program maturity scores, though care must be taken to select indicators that truly reflect strategic priorities rather than just what is easily measured. KPIs showing faster resolution of identified issues, cost savings from proactive risk management, and reduction in violations can be directly tied to the achievement of GRC objectives.

Implementing a feedback loop to continuously refine and improve the alignment between legal strategy and GRC objectives is critical. It should include regular reviews of legal strategy effectiveness, soliciting feedback from stakeholders across the organization, and adapting strategies based on evolving organizational needs and GRC maturity.

Simply put, measuring the success of your efforts and ensuring refinement in your approach when necessary enhance your ability to bring value to the organization.

Elevating Your Role

By aligning legal strategy with GRC objectives, you can elevate your role from solely a legal advisor to a strategic partner in the organization's success. This alignment ensures that legal expertise is leveraged effectively to protect the organization and drive its growth and performance in a compliant and risk-aware manner.

Consider the example of a technology company expanding into new international markets. The general counsel recognizes the need for a more integrated GRC approach to manage the complexities of cross-border operations and has the legal team lead the implementation of a comprehensive GRC framework that integrates risk management, compliance, and governance functions. The team works closely with the CIO and technology team to implement a centralized GRC platform that allows for real-time monitoring of compliance across different jurisdictions. It also collaborates with HR to develop a global code of conduct adaptable to local cultural norms while maintaining consistent ethical standards and coordinates with purchasing to implement a robust third-party due diligence process to manage risks in new markets.

Through these efforts, the company successfully navigates its international expansion with minimal compliance issues. The integrated GRC approach improves decision-making, reduces duplicative efforts, and enhances the company's reputation with regulators and stakeholders. The general counsel also benefits by establishing the legal team as integral to the achievement of business objectives.

Cross-functional Collaboration in GRC: The Lawyer as Leader

In today's business operations, cross-functional collaboration is not just beneficial; it is essential. With your legal perspectives and skills, you are ideally positioned to lead these collaborative efforts. Legal professionals bring distinct value by translating legal requirements into operational terms, providing legal context to risk and compliance decisions, and ensuring legal considerations are integrated into GRC strategies. By spearheading cross-functional initiatives, you can elevate your role from advisor to key driver of organizational success through GRC excellence.

The Imperative of Collaboration

Cross-functional collaboration in GRC involves the coordinated efforts of various departments to achieve comprehensive governance, effective risk management, and robust compliance. As a leader in this space, you should help break down silos and enhance communication between departments, establish and guide a holistic approach to GRC challenges, and facilitate the development and operation of efficient and effective GRC processes.

Unless you are the only lawyer serving as the legal department of your client organization, you will likely specialize in a particular type of law with other lawyers meeting different needs. For example, you might be the lawyer analyzing regulations that must be addressed in third-party relationships, while another lawyer specializes in drafting contracts with third parties, and a third lawyer specializes in third-party due diligence and assessment. If your client organization is a government contractor, there may be yet another lawyer responsible for ensuring compliance with all contractor requirements to avoid debarment. You might need to suggest a particular contract clause that the second lawyer has the responsibility to draft and include in contracts, while the third lawyer needs to ensure compliance with that clause, the fourth lawyer must get involved if any violation of the clause risks the loss of contractor status, and they may need to pull in a litigator. To make this happen smoothly, ongoing collaboration must take place within your legal department or law firm, or between law firms in some cases, to ensure that everyone is on the same page.

Key Stakeholders and Their Roles

Effective collaboration also involves engaging with those who work in:

- **Risk Management:** Assessing and mitigating organizational risks
- **Compliance:** Ensuring adherence to laws, regulations, and internal policies
- **Internal Audit:** Providing independent assurance
- **IT/Cybersecurity:** Managing technology-related risks and compliance
- **Human Resources:** Addressing people-related GRC issues

- **Finance:** Managing financial risks and compliance
- **Operations:** Implementing GRC practices in day-to-day activities
- **Executive Leadership:** Setting the tone and strategy for GRC

Building ongoing relationships and trust with your counterparts in each role leads to greater openness and willingness to share important information at the early stages of business decisions, enabling you to have influence when needed.

Establishing Collaborative Structures and Processes

Lawyers are uniquely positioned to spearhead cross-functional collaboration in GRC. Your legal acumen and holistic understanding of organizational risks and regulatory requirements enable you to initiate and oversee crucial collaborative structures. These may include cross-functional GRC committees and regular interdepartmental meetings, which serve as forums for diverse perspectives and expertise to converge.

Moreover, legal leaders in your client organization can play a pivotal role in selecting shared GRC technology platforms and implementing integrated reporting systems. These technological foundations facilitate seamless information flow and data-driven decision-making across the organization. Once these structures are in place, you can coordinate joint risk assessments, a process that benefits immensely from diverse departmental inputs. You can also oversee integrated policy development and management, ensuring that organizational policies are cohesive and aligned with legal requirements and business objectives.

In the critical area of incident response, you can guide collaborative planning efforts, leveraging your expertise in potential legal ramifications and regulatory obligations. Furthermore, you can ensure that compliance monitoring and reporting processes are cohesive, providing a unified view of the organization's GRC posture.

Overcoming Collaboration Challenges

The path to effective GRC collaboration is often fraught with obstacles, many of which lawyers are well equipped to address. Departmental silos and territorial issues, for instance, can be mitigated through carefully crafted communication strategies and by emphasizing the shared benefits of collaboration. You can also navigate the often-conflicting priorities among stakeholders, using your negotiation skills to find common ground and mutually beneficial solutions.

Another common challenge is inconsistent messaging across the organization, which you can address through the development of clear, unified communication protocols. Your attention to detail and precision in language can ensure that GRC-related messages are consistent, regardless of their point of origin within the organization.

Best Practices for Leading Collaboration

You can employ various best practices to excel in leading GRC collaboration. Facilitating regular cross-functional workshops, for example, can foster a shared understanding of GRC challenges and opportunities. You can align diverse departments toward common objectives by championing shared goal setting and key performance indicators (KPIs).

Promoting cross-training initiatives is another effective strategy. These programs can enhance mutual understanding among different functions and create a more versatile workforce capable of addressing GRC issues from multiple angles. Perhaps most importantly, you should strive to foster a culture of open communication, where concerns can be raised without fear and ideas can flow freely across departmental boundaries.

Measuring Collaborative Success

As with any strategic initiative, the success of GRC collaboration efforts must be measured and evaluated. You can develop and track metrics for collaborative effectiveness, such as the frequency and quality of cross-functional interactions and the level of information sharing among departments.

Furthermore, you can spearhead impact assessments on overall GRC performance. These assessments might examine how collaborative efforts have improved risk mitigation, enhanced compliance adherence, or streamlined governance processes. By quantifying these impacts, you can demonstrate the value of collaboration and make data-driven arguments for continued investment in collaborative structures and processes.

Future Trends in GRC Collaboration

Looking ahead, you and all legal team members must stay attuned to emerging trends that will shape the future of GRC collaboration. Emerging technologies, such as artificial intelligence and blockchain, promise to enhance collaborative efforts by improving data analysis, automating routine tasks, and increasing transparency. Lawyers should be at the forefront of evaluating and implementing these technologies, ensuring they are leveraged effectively and in compliance with relevant regulations.

Additionally, organizational structures are evolving to better support integrated GRC approaches. Legal leaders should be prepared to adapt to and shape these new structures, which may include more matrix-based reporting lines or the creation of dedicated GRC units that span traditional departmental boundaries.

By embracing these trends and continuing to champion cross-functional collaboration, you can cement your role as an indispensable leader in the ever-evolving field of GRC.

The Lawyer as Collaborative Leader

By taking the lead in cross-functional collaboration, you can transform the GRC landscape within your client organization. This leadership role allows you to:

- Drive a more integrated and effective GRC approach
- Enhance the strategic value of the legal function
- Position yourself as an indispensable partner in organizational success

As GRC continues to evolve, lawyers who excel in leading collaborative efforts find themselves at the forefront of organizational strategy and decision-making. Bridging gaps between departments, facilitating shared understanding, and driving cohesive GRC initiatives elevate your impact far beyond traditional legal practice boundaries.

By embracing this leadership role, you enhance the effectiveness of GRC efforts and significantly elevate your strategic importance to the organization. The future of GRC belongs to those who can lead across functions, and lawyers are uniquely positioned to do so.

Legal's Role in Risk Management

Lawyers play a pivotal role in risk management within the GRC framework. Your perspective, honed through years of legal training and practice, allows you to identify, evaluate, and mitigate legal risks that could significantly impact the organization. This role goes far beyond identifying and managing regulatory noncompliance risk; it involves a proactive, strategic approach to managing legal risk as an integral part of the organization's overall risk management strategy.

Risk Identification

The first step in effective risk management is identifying potential risks to the achievement of defined objectives. You bring a unique lens to this process, able to spot legal pitfalls that might escape the notice of other professionals. This begins with comprehensive legal risk audits across various business units. These audits involve in-depth reviews of contracts, operations, and practices to identify areas of potential legal exposure.

You must stay abreast of the ever-changing regulatory landscape. This involves monitoring current laws and regulations and anticipating future changes. For instance, you might identify potential risks arising from proposed data protection legislation, allowing the organization to proactively adjust its practices.

Collaboration is key in this phase. You should work closely with relevant departments to understand their operations and identify potential legal implications. For example, a conversation with the marketing team might reveal a planned campaign that could violate advertising regulations, allowing the legal team to address the issue before it becomes a problem.

Risk Assessment

Once risks are identified, you must work with risk experts to assess the risks for their potential impact. Legal professionals provide context here. You can evaluate the potential consequences of legal risks, from financial penalties to reputational damage, and assess the likelihood of these risks materializing based on your understanding of legal trends, enforcement actions, and precedents.

This assessment should not happen in isolation. You should participate in broader organizational risk assessments, providing the legal perspective alongside financial, operational, and strategic considerations. This holistic approach ensures that legal risks are properly contextualized within the organization's overall risk profile.

A key part of this assessment is evaluating the adequacy of existing controls. You should review current policies, procedures, and safeguards to determine if they provide sufficient protection against identified legal risks. This might involve, for example, assessing whether current contract templates adequately protect the organization's interests or whether existing compliance training is sufficient to mitigate regulatory risks.

Risk Mitigation

After identifying and assessing risks, the next step is developing and implementing mitigation strategies. Here, you can draw on your expertise to craft solutions that effectively manage legal risks while supporting business objectives.

This might involve developing new contractual protections, such as more robust indemnification clauses or clearer limitation of liability provisions. It could also include recommending changes to business processes to reduce legal exposure. For instance, you might suggest modifications to the product development process to ensure proper intellectual property protections are in place from the outset.

In some cases, risk mitigation might involve more sweeping changes. For example, you might recommend restructuring certain business operations to limit liability exposure or advise on the creation of new compliance programs to address arising regulatory risks.

Ongoing Monitoring

Risk management is not a one-time exercise; it is an ongoing process. Legal professionals play a part in continuously monitoring the organization's legal risk profile. This involves establishing and tracking legal key risk indicators (KRIs)—metrics that can provide early warning of increasing legal risk.

You should participate regularly in risk review meetings, providing updates on changes in the legal risk landscape and the effectiveness of current mitigation strategies. This ongoing involvement ensures that legal risk management remains dynamic and responsive to changes in both the organization and its external context.

Crisis Management

Despite the best efforts at prevention, crises arise. In these situations, lawyers play a major role. This begins with developing legal response plans for potential crises, ensuring the organization is prepared to respond swiftly and effectively to legal emergencies.

During a crisis, lawyers provide real-time legal advice, helping guide the organization's response in a way that minimizes legal exposure while addressing the immediate situation. This might involve advising on public statements, managing regulatory inquiries, or coordinating with outside counsel and public relations experts.

After a crisis, you should lead a post-crisis review from a legal perspective. This involves analyzing what happened, assessing the effectiveness of the organization's response, and identifying lessons learned to improve future risk management efforts.

By actively engaging in all aspects of risk management, you can help your client organization proactively address legal risks. This protects the organization from potential harm and supports its strategic objectives by creating a more resilient, risk-aware business. In doing so, you elevate your role from reactive problem solver to proactive strategic partner in the organization's success.

Navigating GRC in Highly Regulated Industries

Certain industries stand out for the intensity and detail of their regulatory schemes. Banking, healthcare, pharmaceuticals, and energy sectors are prime examples of these highly regulated industries. The GRC landscape presents unique challenges to and demands specialized approaches from lawyers working in or advising these sectors.

Intensive Regulatory Oversight

Highly regulated industries are characterized by intensive regulatory oversight, unclear and frequently changing regulations, and severe consequences for noncompliance. These sectors face heightened public and governmental scrutiny, with industry-specific regulatory bodies and frameworks shaping their operational landscape. For instance, banks must navigate a web of financial regulations, from anti–money laundering laws to capital requirements, while healthcare providers grapple with patient privacy rules and quality of care standards.

Lawyers working for highly regulated industries face a distinct set of challenges. Keeping pace with rapid regulatory changes is a constant demand. Healthcare lawyers, for example, might find themselves scrambling to interpret and implement new telemedicine regulations in the wake of a global pandemic. Balancing compliance with business objectives becomes a delicate dance, as strict regulations can sometimes conflict with operational efficiency or growth strategies.

Managing relationships with regulatory bodies takes on heightened importance in these industries. Lawyers are usually the primary liaison between their organization and regulators, requiring legal acumen and diplomatic skills. You must coordinate cross-functional compliance efforts, ensuring that every part of the organization, from operations to finance to human resources, is aligned with regulatory requirements.

Critical Controls

Implementing robust documentation and reporting systems is essential. For example, maintaining detailed records of clinical trials and adverse event reporting in the pharmaceutical industry is not just good practice; it is a regulatory mandate with significant legal implications.

Highly regulated industries' focus areas include strict governance structures, enhanced risk management protocols, and comprehensive compliance programs. Internal controls take on added significance, with detailed reporting and disclosure requirements often mandated by law. A banking lawyer, for instance, might be deeply involved in designing and implementing controls to prevent insider trading or ensure compliance with Basel III capital requirements.[1]

Regulatory Change Management

Lawyers in highly regulated industries must develop several key strategies to navigate these waters. First and foremost is the cultivation of deep, industry-specific regulatory knowledge. This goes beyond understanding the letter of the law to grasp its practical implications and the regulators' enforcement priorities.

Implementing proactive regulatory monitoring systems is essential. Many law departments in these industries employ dedicated teams that use advanced software solutions and services to track regulatory changes and assess their potential impact. Fostering strong relationships with regulatory bodies while maintaining appropriate boundaries can also provide valuable insights and facilitate smoother interactions during audits or investigations.

Creating agile compliance frameworks that can swiftly adapt to regulatory changes is essential. This might involve developing modular compliance programs that can be quickly updated or leveraging technology for compliance management and reporting. For example, a healthcare lawyer might champion the adoption of AI-powered tools to monitor patient data privacy compliance in real time.

Most importantly, lawyers in these industries play a key role in cultivating a strong culture of compliance throughout their organizations. This involves drafting policies, conducting training sessions, and working with leadership to embed compliance considerations into the organization's decision-making processes at every level.

Balance of Goals

The interplay between industry-specific regulations and broader GRC principles presents both challenges and opportunities. You must find ways to align industry regulations with the overall GRC framework, identify synergies where possible, and manage potential conflicts. For

[1] https://www.bis.org/basel_framework/index.htm.

instance, an energy sector lawyer might need to reconcile specific environmental regulations with broader corporate sustainability goals and operational expansion plans. Highly regulated organizations may have hundreds of people in a compliance group tasked with ensuring industry-specific regulatory compliance yet have no one actively integrating the activities of that group or the data it uses with the broader GRC capability of the organization. This is a big mistake.

Consider a scenario in which a multinational bank is implementing a new digital payment system. The legal team must navigate a web of regulations, from data protection laws in multiple jurisdictions to anti–money laundering requirements. They must work closely with IT, operations, and compliance teams to ensure the new system meets all regulatory requirements while still delivering the desired business benefits. The lawyer must perform a multifaceted job in which legal, technical, and business considerations are inextricably linked.

In highly regulated industries, the role of lawyers has already widely evolved from legal advisors to strategic partners in the business. They balance deep technical legal expertise with broad business acumen, leading cross-functional compliance initiatives. Increasingly, they are also called upon to drive innovation in GRC practices, finding new ways to meet regulatory requirements more efficiently and effectively.

The Road Ahead

Looking ahead, the landscape for GRC in highly regulated industries continues to evolve. Emerging technologies like blockchain and artificial intelligence are presenting new regulatory challenges and opportunities. Increased focus on data privacy and environmental sustainability is expanding the scope of regulation in many industries. Climate-related financial disclosures, for instance, are a key concern for lawyers in the banking and energy sectors, especially in the EU, where regulatory requirements are expanding.

It is clear that navigating GRC in highly regulated industries requires a specialized skill set and approach. Lawyers in these sectors must be adept at managing regulatory requirements, fostering a culture of compliance, and balancing risk management with business objectives. As regulations continue to evolve and increase in complexity, the role of lawyers in shaping effective GRC strategies in these industries will only grow in importance. Those who can master these challenges will find themselves playing a valued role in their client organization's success and integrity.

Cross-Border Integration of Legal Expertise in GRC

In today's globalized business setting, the integration of legal expertise across borders has become a critical component of effective GRC strategy. As organizations expand internationally, they face a web of diverse legal systems, regulatory frameworks, and cultural norms. You must effectively integrate your expertise across jurisdictions to support a cohesive yet flexible global GRC framework.

Understanding the Challenges of Cross-Border Legal Integration

The integration of legal expertise across borders presents several unique challenges. Organizations must reconcile different regulatory philosophies, from principles-based to rules-based systems, while maintaining consistency in their GRC approach. They must also simultaneously navigate the fundamental differences between common law, civil law, and other legal frameworks that shape everything from contract formation to dispute resolution mechanisms.

These challenges are further complicated by cultural and ethical variations that affect what constitutes acceptable business practice, while language barriers can create significant risks when legal concepts don't translate clearly across jurisdictions. Adding another layer of complexity is the growing prevalence of extraterritorial laws like the US Foreign Corrupt Practices Act (FCPA) and the EU's General Data Protection Regulation (GDPR), which extend their reach beyond traditional borders and require organizations to comply with multiple overlapping regulatory regimes regardless of their home jurisdiction.

Strategies for Effective Cross-Border Legal Integration

To address these challenges and effectively integrate legal expertise across borders, lawyers should consider the following strategies:

- **Develop a Global Legal Network:** Establish a network of local legal experts in each jurisdiction where the organization operates. This network can provide invaluable insights into local laws, customs, and business practices.
- **Create a Global-Local Balance:** Develop a GRC framework that sets global standards while allowing for necessary local adaptations. This "glocal" approach ensures consistency in core principles while respecting local legal and cultural nuances.
- **Implement Cross-Border Legal Teams:** Form international legal teams that bring together expertise from different jurisdictions. These teams can collaborate on cross-border issues and share best practices.
- **Leverage Technology:** Use legal tech solutions, such as global contract management systems or international compliance tracking tools, that can handle multi-jurisdictional requirements.
- **Enhance Cross-Cultural Competence:** Invest in training to develop cross-cultural competence among legal teams. This includes understanding different negotiation styles, communication norms, and business practices across cultures.
- **Standardize Processes Where Possible:** Develop standardized processes for common legal activities (e.g., contract review, compliance reporting) that can be adapted to local requirements as needed.
- **Regular Cross-Border Legal Reviews:** Conduct periodic reviews of the organization's legal positions across all jurisdictions to identify potential conflicts or opportunities for harmonization.
- **Develop a Global Risk Assessment Framework:** Create a risk assessment methodology that considers legal and regulatory risks across all relevant jurisdictions, allowing for a comprehensive view of the organization's global risk profile.

Consider the example of a multinational corporation expanding its operations into Southeast Asia. You might begin cross-border integration by establishing a regional legal hub in Singapore, with local legal experts hired in each country. Next, you could develop a core set of compliance policies that apply company wide, with appendices for country-specific requirements, and implement a global contract management system with clauses for different jurisdictions.

As you operate, you might conduct regular video conferences between global and local legal teams to discuss emerging issues and share knowledge. You also could provide cultural competence training for all legal team members, focusing on Asian business practices and legal systems.

By creating a standardized due diligence process for new business partners, with additional checks for high-risk jurisdictions, and implementing a quarterly legal review process that examines the company's legal positions across all Asian operations to identify any cross-border issues or conflicts, you could ensure effective oversight and identification of necessary program changes.

Effective cross-border integration of legal expertise is essential for organizations operating in multiple jurisdictions. By developing a robust global-local approach, leveraging technology, fostering cross-cultural competence, and maintaining open communication channels, legal teams can create a GRC framework that is both globally consistent and locally relevant. This integrated approach enhances compliance and risk management and positions the legal team as a valuable strategic partner in the organization's global operations.

Conclusion

Integrating legal expertise and experience across the GRC framework can significantly enhance an organization's ability to navigate risks, ensure compliance, and achieve its strategic objectives. By aligning legal strategy with business objectives, fostering cross-functional collaboration, and balancing legal considerations with GRC objectives, you can elevate your role from advisor to strategic partner. The challenges are numerous, particularly in highly regulated industries, but so are the opportunities for lawyers to drive value and innovation. As the GRC landscape continues to evolve, lawyers who successfully integrate their expertise across the framework are well-positioned to lead their organizations toward sustainable success and resilience.

Action Items

- Conduct a gap analysis of your organization's current GRC framework to identify areas where legal expertise can be better integrated.

- Develop a cross-functional collaboration plan, identifying key stakeholders from different departments for regular GRC meetings.
- Develop a framework for balancing legal considerations with business objectives.
- Recommend and manage a process for regular legal input in strategic decision-making, such as a legal review stage for major business initiatives.
- Design a communication strategy to articulate the value of legal expertise in GRC to senior management and the board.

Interview with Son-U Michael Paik

CEO of GRC Solutions Korea

"OCEG's GRC Capability Model and other materials are better than an MBA for 'real world' skills and knowledge."

Switzer: Thirty years ago, you earned an MBA from Yale and a JD from Columbia University. Since then, you've held a number of impressive legal and business roles in the US and in South Korea, where now you are the founder and CEO of GRC Solutions Korea. Tell me a bit about your journey and how you came to advocate GRC for Korean businesses.

Paik: The short version is that I started my practice in New York on Wall Street and then moved to California with the first dot-com boom. There, my work mostly involved technology companies and their investors and some public company M&A activity. When I moved back to Seoul, Korea, I transitioned to developing in-house legal and compliance systems for globally active companies based in Asia.

These companies had evolved in a very different environment, with close government supervision and support. Their systems were entirely focused on compliance with local laws and risk management vis-à-vis

(*Continued*)

the Korean government rather than counterparties and the market. As they have grown in scale and breadth, it's become increasingly clear that they need those latter capabilities as well as improved governance to address the needs of stakeholders beyond the owners and government. It's taking some time, but the direction is clear.

There were several iterations of how I sought to drive this expansion of capability before I found OCEG and the GRC Capability Model. I started very simply, deploying the due diligence [DD] checklists I had used in corporate practice to diagnose, triage, and then address internal issues in an inverted DD process and then started to develop resources, systems, and tools for managing issues. I then focused on operations for efficiency gains, using the Association of Corporate Counsel [ACC] model. Finally, I used enterprise risk management [ERM] for continuous improvement and value creation, using methods such as bow tie analysis for designing and building systems for managing compliance.

I worked with COSO and various ISO management systems and took many courses and certifications before I discovered OCEG's GRC Capability Model on the internet. It addressed everything that I had studied, worked on, iterated on, and more, and it had beautiful graphics!

I was hooked from the beginning and trained my legal, compliance, and trade teams, as well as the CEO and majority shareholder at my last in-house position on OCEG's GRC Capability Model. I reached out to OCEG to see whether they'd be interested in developing a Korean translation, as I believe that there's a [dire] need for it in this part of the world for the reasons noted [earlier]. We did develop the Korean model together, and now I offer training and consulting in APAC, augmented also with AI apps for risk and compliance management.

Switzer: How has the development of GRC as a business management approach affected your work as a lawyer?

Paik: I have found that in-house lawyers really need systems for risk and compliance management, and the GRC Capability Model is a very efficient and comprehensive means of designing, building, and then deploying these management systems in the corporate context.

Most lawyers, especially those in law firms, focus only on boundary conditions, whether voluntary (e.g., policies and contracts) or mandatory (e.g., legal or regulatory regimes). While they have subject matter expertise in those areas, most of them have no idea how these issues should be managed in the corporate context, where this work needs to be integrated with other departments.

GRC addresses this need for systems, and what I like about the OCEG approach is that it's easily integrated with ISO standards as well as ESG agendas and projects. For lawyers, it enables close cooperation with compliance and other functions in developing and deploying management systems. It's a handbook that sets out a step-by-step approach that can be used for anything ranging from managing a post-merger integration to building a whistleblower policy or an export control compliance management system. I have used it for these applications and more.

The GRC Capability Model outlines the core components and elements that comprise capabilities that can be used to build systems that create pathways to Principled Performance. Principled Performance is a concept developed by OCEG that encompasses an organization's ability to reliably achieve objectives, address uncertainty, and act with integrity.

These GRC capabilities can be used to build governance, management, and auditing systems. The model consists of four components (learn, align, perform, and review), each of which is described along with considerations and the elements required for each. Twenty elements are distributed among the four components (four for learn, five for align, eight for perform, and three for review), and each element is described along with practices and considerations impacting decisions, design, and operation, as well as tools and techniques.

To build a management system using this model, you simply choose a starting point as described in the model: SP0: Blank Canvas, SP1: Topical, SP2: Discipline, SP3: Element, or SP4: Crisis, and then go through the process, step by step, to build or improve the capabilities required of the system, which will then be deployed as a pathway to Principled Performance. Multiple systems can use and leverage these integrated capabilities for governance, management, and auditing, so building or improving them affects all these systems. I also use this process for designing relevant AI apps.

(*Continued*)

Switzer: What strengths do you think lawyers bring to GRC advisory or in-house roles, and what skill development might they need to address?

Paik: Most lawyers have one analysis process (IRAC) that they deploy into a subject for which they've developed expertise. This may be sufficient for practice in law firms, though their long-term success may also depend on client origination and management, which require interpersonal skills and savvy.

For in-house lawyers and GRC advisors, these interpersonal skills and savvy are also important, as are systems thinking, a greater understanding of the business context, and, increasingly, use of technology.

The most important skill set relates to management, and here is where the GRC Capability Model is very useful, much better than an MBA, really, in understanding "real" governance and management.

Finally, I would note that most of the work for in-house lawyers, especially as you progress through the ranks, is about managing projects, people, processes, resources, and systems. If you don't figure this out early, you will not progress beyond practicing as a subject matter expert, which may be better suited to law firm practice. That said, your organization will expect you to have subject matter expertise as well, and it's imperative that you get those basics covered before you evolve these other skills.

Switzer: How do you see GRC education and certifications being valuable to lawyers who work in house, in government, or in law firms?

Paik: As I've noted, OCEG's GRC Capability Model and other materials are better than an MBA for "real world" skills and knowledge. I have taken all the OCEG certifications and cannot recommend them more highly. They are useful for developing systems thinking and a broader understanding of the corporate context. If you are considering in-house practice or are already there, it's an ideal means for improving your skills in management as you progress in your career. The skills are transferable, and the frameworks will help in integrating your expertise so that data and intelligence become wisdom and experience, which is where long-term value lies.

Chapter 2
Core GRC Roles for Lawyers

Introduction

The role of lawyers in GRC has evolved significantly, expanding beyond being a traditional legal advisor to encompass a wide range of strategic and operational responsibilities. Today, you can hold a number of multifaceted roles in an organization's GRC framework, from providing an understanding of the operational context of the business as it changes over time to driving continuous improvement in GRC processes. You can contribute to each aspect of GRC, bringing unique value even while facing challenges. By understanding these diverse roles, you can better position yourself as indispensable partners in your client organization's GRC efforts.

Evaluating the Operational Context of the Business

GRC professionals must ensure the organization can navigate its operating context locally and globally. Understanding the external context, internal context, organizational culture, and stakeholder expectations is foundational to establishing objectives and strategies to achieve them. In today's interconnected world, this understanding must extend beyond national borders to encompass the global landscape in which many organizations operate, have third-party vendors, or serve customers.

Lawyers, particularly those in senior in-house roles like general counsel, play a crucial role. Their involvement spans from analyzing legal and regulatory aspects of the external context to shaping internal governance structures and fostering a culture of compliance across diverse geographical and cultural contexts.

Examining the External Context

Examining and understanding the context in which the organization operates provides essential information. This involves analyzing various external factors,[1] identifying those the organization may influence, assigning accountability for monitoring these factors, and continuously sensing changes in the external context. In a global operation, this examination becomes quite challenging.

Lawyers play a significant role in assessing legal, regulatory, and political factors across multiple jurisdictions. A legal team typically leads the analysis of current and emerging legislation, regulations, administrative rulings, agency guidance, and judicial opinions that could impact the organization. When a multinational business or organization is the client, this analysis must extend to understanding varying regulatory approaches in different regions. For instance, while the United States favors a rules-based approach with specific, detailed regulations, many European countries adopt a principles-based approach, providing broader guidelines that companies must interpret and apply.

In-house counsel frequently collaborates with government relations teams to understand political factors, while outside counsel may be engaged for specialized expertise in specific jurisdictions or emerging areas of law. This collaboration becomes particularly important when navigating the complexities of cross-border compliance issues.

Lawyers, especially those specializing in government relations, play a key role in shaping external factors in efforts to influence the external context. This might involve participating in industry associations, providing input on proposed regulations, or engaging in lobbying activities. In a global context, this could extend to engaging with international regulatory bodies or contributing to the development of global standards.

Senior legal leaders are often assigned accountability for monitoring and responding to specific legal and regulatory factors. They typically

[1] The GRC Glossary defines external factors as categories of sources and forces that originate outside the organization, including industry, market, economic, technology, societal, legal, political, environmental, and demographic factors (https://www.oceg.org/glossary).

work in tandem with other C-suite executives and department heads to ensure a comprehensive approach to external context analysis. This responsibility includes staying informed about regulatory changes across all relevant jurisdictions and developing agile processes to quickly adapt to new requirements.

Lawyers contribute significantly to continuously monitoring the external context by setting up alert systems, subscribing to legal updates and specialized update services, or leveraging outside counsel networks to stay informed about relevant developments. For a global organization, this might involve building a network of local legal and compliance experts in each jurisdiction. Their insights into local laws, customs, and business practices are invaluable.

Legal teams play a key role in defining triggers for reassessing the external context, particularly legal and regulatory factors. They may set up periodic reviews of the legal landscape or identify specific events, such as major court decisions or the passage of new laws, which would necessitate reassessing the organization's strategies or operations. In a global context, these triggers must be sensitive to international events and regulatory shifts that could impact the organization's operations across multiple countries.

If you are involved in these activities, you typically work closely with other GRC professionals in strategy, risk management, and government relations. While you may lead efforts related to legal and regulatory factors, you may also serve as an advisor or contributor in other areas, providing legal perspectives on how various external factors might impact the organization's operations and strategy. This collaborative approach is particularly crucial when dealing with international operations, where legal, cultural, and business factors are closely intertwined.

Examining the Internal Context

Examining and understanding how the organization is structured and operating is equally essential, especially in the context of global operations. This involves analyzing internal strengths and weaknesses, identifying factors that can be influenced, assigning accountability for managing key internal factors,[2] continuously monitoring changes, and defining triggers for reassessment.

Lawyers, particularly in-house counsel, play a significant role in this activity. They are essential contributors to analyzing the internal context, especially when it comes to assessing organizational structures, policies, and processes. Legal team members contribute significantly to policy development and review. They analyze how internal factors align with legal and regulatory requirements, frequently collaborating with HR, compliance, and operations teams to ensure a comprehensive understanding of the internal context.

In a global organization, this evaluation must consider how internal structures and processes accommodate different regulatory requirements and business practices across countries. For instance, data protection policies must be designed to comply with requirements such as the EU's GDPR and China's data localization laws.

When it comes to influencing the internal context, you can be an influential advisor and sometimes a leader in shaping internal factors. This might involve drafting or revising corporate policies, contributing to the development of ethical guidelines, or advising on the legal implications of proposed changes to organizational structures or processes. In a global context, this could include developing global policies that set consistent standards while allowing for necessary local adaptations.

Senior legal leaders may be assigned accountability for certain internal factors, particularly those directly related to governance, ethics, and compliance. They typically work in tandem with other executives to ensure a coordinated approach to managing the internal context. This might involve collaborating with regional legal teams to ensure consistent governance practices across different jurisdictions in multinational corporations.

In monitoring the internal context, lawyers contribute by tracking changes that may have legal implications. This might involve regular reviews of corporate policies, participation in cross-functional meetings, or setting up reporting mechanisms to stay informed about significant

---

[2] The GRC Glossary defines internal factors as categories of sources and forces that originate inside the organization (https://www.oceg.org/glossary). These include organizational structure, subcultures, technologies in use, established practices and policies, and other factors that may shift over time.

internal developments. In-house lawyers collaborate with compliance officers, internal audit teams, and HR to ensure timely awareness of relevant internal changes. For global organizations, this monitoring must be sensitive to how changes in one region might impact operations or compliance in another.

Lawyers also define triggers for reassessing the internal context, particularly for governance- and compliance-related factors. This could involve setting up periodic reviews of internal policies and procedures or identifying specific events, such as leadership changes or major reorganizations, that would necessitate a reassessment of the organization's internal context. In a global setting, these triggers might also include significant changes in local regulations or business environments that could necessitate adjustments to global policies or practices.

Throughout these activities, you typically work closely with GRC professionals in various departments, including HR, finance, operations, and strategy. While you may lead efforts related to governance and compliance aspects of the internal context, you also serve as an advisor or contributor in other areas, providing legal perspectives on how various internal factors might impact the organization's risk profile, compliance status, and overall operations.

The general counsel or another senior lawyer might also serve as the corporate secretary, playing a crucial role in maintaining corporate records and ensuring proper governance procedures. In this capacity, you would be deeply involved in understanding and shaping the organization's internal context, particularly in areas related to board operations and corporate governance. In a multinational corporation, this role might involve ensuring that governance practices are consistent across different jurisdictions while complying with local requirements.

Assessing and Building Organizational Culture

Lawyers too often ignore the need to truly understand the existing culture, climate, and mindsets about governance, assurance, and management of performance, risk, and compliance within the organization. It is fair to say that lawyers, particularly in-house counsel, play a narrower direct role in organizational culture analysis than they might in external and internal context analysis. Nevertheless, you can play a key role in analyzing the organization's culture across several dimensions, including compliance culture, risk culture, ethical culture, governance culture, and workforce culture.

In-house counsel, working closely with compliance officers, contributes to understanding how the workforce and third parties perceive and fulfill mandatory and voluntary obligations. In this role, you provide insights into how well legal and regulatory requirements are understood and adhered to across the extended enterprise. In a global context, this involves understanding how compliance attitudes and behaviors might vary across diverse cultural contexts and developing strategies to foster a consistent compliance culture worldwide.

Legal team members contribute to developing and promoting ethical standards within the organization by examining the ethical culture. Working in conjunction with ethics officers or committees, you can help analyze how well these standards are understood and followed. For multinational corporations, this involves developing a global code of conduct that sets consistent ethical standards while being sensitive to local cultural norms.

When it comes to analyzing governance culture, lawyers, particularly those serving as corporate secretaries, may contribute to understanding how the governing authority and executive team are engaged in governance practices. They can provide insights into whether leadership models appropriate behavior in words and deeds from a legal and governance perspective. In a global organization, this might involve ensuring that governance practices are consistent across different regions while adapting to local regulatory requirements and business norms.

Legal department members assigned accountability for cultural factors typically work with HR, ethics officers, and other relevant departments to monitor and influence these aspects of organizational culture. In efforts to influence culture, you may advise on legal and ethical aspects of culture change initiatives, ensuring that efforts to influence culture align with legal requirements and best practices in corporate governance. For global organizations, this might involve developing training programs that address both global standards and local nuances and encouraging a speak-up culture that transcends geographical boundaries.

You might also contribute to continuously monitoring cultural changes, helping identify legal or ethical issues that could signal cultural shifts requiring attention. You can assist in defining events or timescales that should trigger a reassessment of organizational culture, particularly in areas related to compliance and ethics. In a global context, this monitoring should be sensitive to how cultural changes in one region might impact the broader organization.

It is important to note that lawyers in primarily legal roles typically play a more advisory part rather than leading the analysis of many aspects of organizational culture, such as performance culture, risk culture, or workforce culture. HR, risk management, and operational teams primarily handle these areas, with legal input sought as needed. Lawyers work collaboratively with other departments throughout these activities, providing a legal and ethical perspective on cultural issues. While your role in shaping overall organizational culture may be more limited, your input may be crucial in ensuring your client organization's culture supports compliance with legal and ethical standards across all jurisdictions where the organization operates.

Navigating International GRC Landscapes

In today's interconnected global economy, understanding and navigating international GRC landscapes are crucial for lawyers working in multinational corporations or advising clients with international operations or customers. This involves grappling with a wide range of international regulations, cultural differences, and varying business practices.

Key aspects of the global GRC landscape include:

- **Varying Regulatory Approaches:** Different regions have fundamentally different approaches to regulation. Understanding these differences is crucial for developing effective global GRC strategies.
- **Cross-Border Compliance Challenges:** Companies operating across borders must comply with regulations in multiple jurisdictions, which can sometimes conflict. You must be adept at reconciling these potential conflicts and developing compliance strategies that work across all relevant jurisdictions.
- **Cultural and Ethical Differences:** What is considered ethical business practice in one country might be viewed differently in another. You must be sensitive to these cultural nuances while maintaining consistent ethical standards.
- **Extraterritorial Application of Laws:** Some laws, such as the US Foreign Corrupt Practices Act (FCPA) and the UK Bribery Act,

have extraterritorial reach. You must understand the implications of these laws for your client organization's global operations.

Effective global GRC requires lawyers to develop strategies that balance global consistency with local requirements. This might involve:

- **Developing a Global GRC Framework:** Creating a comprehensive GRC framework for the organization that sets global standards while allowing for necessary local adaptation.
- **Implementing Robust Due Diligence Processes:** Developing thorough due diligence procedures for entering new markets, engaging with third parties, and in M&A activities.
- **Leveraging Technology:** Utilizing GRC technologies that support multijurisdictional requirements.
- **Fostering a Global Compliance Culture:** Developing training programs that address both global standards and local nuances.
- **Collaborating with Local Experts:** Building a network of local legal and compliance experts in each jurisdiction.

By embracing these strategies, you can help your client organization comply with diverse regulatory requirements and thrive in the global marketplace.

Listening to Stakeholders

Both in-house and external lawyers play a significant role in stakeholder management, particularly when it comes to certain types of stakeholders and specific legal or regulatory aspects of stakeholder relationships. You may directly or indirectly interact with stakeholders to understand their expectations, requirements, and perspectives that impact the organization. This involves identifying and prioritizing stakeholders, developing relationships and influence strategies, assigning accountability for stakeholder management, continuously monitoring changes in stakeholder dynamics, and defining triggers for reassessment.

Lawyers play particularly important roles in managing relationships with specific stakeholder groups. They lead interactions with government agencies and regulators, play a crucial role in shareholder communications for public companies, negotiate with creditors and lenders, work closely with the board of directors, and may be heavily involved in managing relationships with unions. Outside counsel may be engaged to provide specialized expertise in dealing with specific stakeholder groups, particularly those in regulatory bodies or jurisdictions where the organization lacks in-house expertise.

In a global context, stakeholder management becomes even more challenging, as stakeholder expectations and engagement practices can vary significantly across diverse cultures and regulatory schemes. You must be adept at navigating these differences while maintaining consistent ethical and legal standards.

Lawyers contribute to the process of identifying stakeholders by helping recognize legal and regulatory stakeholders, such as government agencies, regulators, and potentially litigious groups. You may have insights into which stakeholders may have legal implications for the organization. In a multinational corporation, you may need to map stakeholders across different jurisdictions to understand their varying levels of influence and interest.

When it comes to prioritizing stakeholder needs, you can provide valuable input on the legal risks and obligations associated with different stakeholders. You can help balance stakeholder needs based on legal requirements and potential legal impacts, working closely with other senior leaders to ensure a comprehensive prioritization approach. In a global context, this prioritization must consider how stakeholder influence and importance might vary across different countries and regions.

Lawyers, particularly those in government-relations roles or with specific regulatory expertise, may lead in developing relationships with and influencing certain stakeholders. This is especially true for regulatory bodies and government agencies. They may also advise on communication strategies to ensure legal compliance and risk mitigation when addressing stakeholder concerns. For multinational corporations, this might involve developing strategies for engaging with international regulatory bodies or managing relationships with government stakeholders across multiple jurisdictions.

Both in-house and outside counsel might manage relationships with legal and regulatory stakeholders. The general counsel might also be involved in stakeholder management at the board and executive level, particularly in matters relating to corporate governance and shareholder relations. In a global organization, this could involve coordinating stakeholder engagement strategies across different regions to ensure consistency while adapting to local norms and requirements.

You might contribute to continuous stakeholder monitoring by tracking changes in legal and regulatory stakeholders, such as shifts in regulatory agency leadership or enforcement priorities. You may also help identify emerging stakeholder groups that could have legal implications for the organization. In an international context, this monitoring must be sensitive to geopolitical changes and shifts in the global regulatory landscape that could impact stakeholder relationships.

You can help define triggers for reassessing stakeholder relationships, particularly for legal and regulatory stakeholders. This could involve setting up periodic reviews of the regulatory landscape or identifying specific events that would necessitate a reassessment. For global organizations, these triggers might include significant changes in international trade relations, major regulatory reforms in key markets, or shifts in global public opinion on issues relevant to the organization's operations.

Throughout these activities, you typically work closely with other departments, such as public relations, investor relations, and government affairs. While you may lead efforts related to legal and regulatory stakeholders, you sometimes serve as an advisor or contributor in managing relationships with other stakeholder groups, providing legal perspectives on how various stakeholder interactions might impact the organization's risk profile and legal position.

In a global context, managing these stakeholder relationships becomes even more important. You must be adept at navigating cultural differences in communication and relationship-building, understanding varying expectations of corporate behavior across different societies, and managing potentially conflicting stakeholder demands across different jurisdictions.

While lawyers may not manage all stakeholder relationships, your role is crucial in ensuring that stakeholder interactions are legally sound, compliant with regulations, and aligned with the organization's risk management strategy. In an increasingly globalized business environment, this role extends to helping the organization maintain consistent ethical standards and legal compliance across diverse cultural and regulatory landscapes.

SUMMARY: UNDERSTANDING THE BUSINESS CONTEXT

These points summarize the most important tasks undertaken by lawyers to ensure a complete understanding of the status and changes in the business context:

- Analyze and interpret legal and regulatory aspects of the external context, including monitoring changes in laws and judicial opinions
- Advise on potential legal impacts of external factors on organizational strategy and operations
- Lead interactions with regulatory bodies and government agencies
- Contribute to internal policy development and review, ensuring alignment with legal and regulatory requirements
- Advise on legal implications of organizational structure changes and maintaining corporate governance procedures
- Analyze and promote compliance culture within the organization, including contributing to the development and assessment of ethical standards
- Provide insights on governance practices and leadership behavior from a legal perspective
- Identify, prioritize, and manage relationships with legal and regulatory stakeholders
- Advise on legal risks and obligations associated with different stakeholders, including shareholders and regulatory bodies
- Help define triggers for a reassessment of external context, internal context, international needs, culture, and stakeholder relationships from a legal standpoint

Designing an Aligned Business Plan

The leaders of any organization must define its direction and objectives and design an approach to address opportunities, obstacles, and obligations as they arise. This is crucial in setting the organization's course and ensuring all efforts align with its overall mission and goals.

Well-run organizations establish their mission, vision, and values; set measurable objectives; identify and analyze potential impacts on these objectives; and design strategies to achieve them while managing risks and ensuring compliance. They do so based on their understanding of the context in which the organization is operating and then design the actions and controls that support the objectives.

Lawyers play a vital advisory role, especially those in senior positions such as general counsel, C-suite titles, or corporate secretary. In this role, you can ensure that the organization's direction, objectives, and strategies align with legal and regulatory requirements while contributing to risk management and compliance considerations. Your involvement helps integrate legal and ethical considerations into the core of the organization's strategic planning and decision-making processes.

In SMEs, lawyers often need to wear multiple hats within the GRC framework. Unlike large corporations with dedicated teams for each GRC function, SMEs may rely on a single legal advisor to cover multiple aspects of governance, risk management, and compliance. This requires you to be particularly versatile and efficient in your approach. For instance, you might need to develop a streamlined compliance program covering essential regulatory requirements while advising on risk management and corporate governance issues. The challenge lies in creating a robust GRC framework that is proportionate to the SME's size and risk profile without overwhelming its resources or hindering its agility.

Providing Clear Direction

Leaders must guide the organization with a clear mission, vision, and values statement that shapes overall goals and strategies. This process involves defining direction-setting criteria, creating formal statements about the organization's purpose and aspirations, selecting and prioritizing stakeholders, exploring and selecting goals and strategies, and establishing processes for validating and reconsidering the direction.

Lawyers, particularly those in senior roles such as general counsel, play a significant advisory role in setting the organization's direction. While they typically are not the primary decision-makers, their input is crucial in ensuring that the direction aligns with legal and ethical standards.

Lawyers ensure that legal and regulatory considerations are incorporated in defining direction-setting criteria. When setting the organization's course, you may advise how to factor in compliance obligations and legal risks. This helps create a framework for decision-making that balances business objectives with legal requirements.

When it comes to defining the organization's mission, vision, and values, lawyers often are involved in drafting or reviewing these statements. The general counsel or a lawyer serving as the compliance and ethics officer might work closely with the C-suite and board to incorporate principles of integrity and compliance into the organization's core values, ensuring that ethical and legal considerations are at the heart of the organization's identity.

When a governance team at any level is exploring and selecting goals and strategies, you can provide valuable input on the legal implications and risks associated with different strategic options. This helps ensure that chosen strategies align with regulatory requirements and the organization's risk tolerance. Your involvement also prevents the adoption of strategies that could expose the organization to undue legal risk.

You may also be involved in the validation process, particularly when explaining the chosen direction's legal and compliance aspects to various organizational units. Your role in this communication process helps ensure that all parts of the organization understand the strategic direction's legal and ethical implications. You may also contribute to defining triggers for reconsidering the organization's direction, particularly those related to significant legal or regulatory changes that could impact the viability of the current strategy.

Throughout this process, you typically work closely with the C-suite, the board of directors, and other senior leaders. While you may not lead the direction-setting process, your input ensures that legal and ethical considerations are integrated into the organization's mission, vision, values, and strategic goals. This helps create a foundation for the organization that is not only ambitious and forward-looking but also legally sound and ethically grounded.

Defining Objective-Setting Criteria

Lawyers have a key supportive role in defining a balanced set of measurable objectives, results, and indicators for the organization. This process involves establishing criteria for setting, exploring, and selecting objectives; defining measurable indicators; assigning accountability; and creating processes for validating and reconsidering objectives.

While the primary leadership typically comes from senior executives, department heads, and strategic planning teams, you can play an important advisory role. You should contribute to defining objective-setting criteria by advising on the inclusion of legal and compliance considerations. This helps ensure that the framework for setting objectives considers legal risks, regulatory requirements, and other business factors.

When exploring and selecting objectives, you should provide input on various proposed objectives' legal risks and compliance requirements. Your insights help ensure that the chosen objectives align with regulatory obligations and the organization's risk tolerance. This is particularly crucial when objectives relate to entering new markets, launching new products, or making significant operational changes.

In the process of defining indicators and results, you might contribute to establishing compliance-related metrics. These could include indicators related to regulatory compliance rates, resolution of legal issues, or other measures crucial for monitoring the organization's legal and regulatory standing.

While lawyers are typically not responsible for assigning objectives to individuals or departments, they themselves may be assigned objectives related to legal and compliance matters. For example, the general counsel or legal department might be given objectives related to maintaining compliance rates, managing legal risks, or achieving certain legal outcomes.

In the validation process for objectives, you may review and approve them to ensure they do not conflict with legal or regulatory requirements. This step helps prevent the organization from pursuing objectives that could lead to legal complications. You might also contribute to defining events or circumstances that would necessitate reconsidering objectives, particularly those related to significant changes in the legal or regulatory environment.

Throughout this process, you work closely with other leaders, providing a legal and compliance perspective that helps integrate these considerations into the organization's operational goals. Your involvement ensures that the organization's objectives are not only ambitious and aligned with the overall strategy but also legally sound and compliant with relevant regulations.

Identifying Opportunities, Obstacles, and Obligations

Lawyers have a primary role in imagining, identifying, and describing the opportunities, obstacles, and obligations that might impact the organization's objectives. This process involves setting identification criteria, understanding the existing approach, systematically identifying a range of factors that could affect the organization's strategies, and prioritizing these for further analysis.

Lawyers, particularly those specializing in compliance or risk management, play a significant role in this identification process. At the outset, they contribute to defining the criteria for identifying and prioritizing opportunities, obstacles, and obligations. This includes helping establish targets, appetites, tolerances, and capacities, especially in areas related to legal and compliance risks.

Legal teams provide valuable insights into compliance controls and potential legal gaps when reviewing and mapping the existing context, direction, objectives, and strategies. In this role, you work alongside operational and risk managers to understand how current approaches might introduce new opportunities, obstacles, or obligations from a legal perspective.

While strategy teams typically lead in identifying opportunities and associated rewards, lawyers play a crucial role in identifying obstacles and levels of risk, particularly those related to legal and regulatory challenges. You are at the forefront of identifying mandatory and voluntary obligations and assessing compliance levels associated with existing and proposed strategies. This is an area where legal expertise is paramount, as lawyers can navigate different regulatory landscapes and anticipate potential compliance issues.

Lawyers also contribute to identifying how assorted opportunities, obstacles, and obligations are interrelated and influenced by each other. Their broad perspective on legal and regulatory trends helps in understanding how these factors might interact and impact the organization's objectives.

Senior legal leaders play a key role in communicating and finalizing the identified legal and compliance-related items with other organizational units in the validation process. They help ensure that all relevant legal and regulatory considerations are properly accounted for and understood across the organization. When it comes to prioritizing opportunities, obstacles, and obligations for further analysis, you provide crucial input on the importance and potential impact of legal and compliance issues. You also help balance these considerations against other business priorities.

Throughout this identification process, legal teams may suggest modifications to objectives based on the legal risks or obligations they have identified. You work closely with business leaders to ensure the organization's goals remain achievable within the legal and regulatory framework. You also may contribute to defining events or timescales that should trigger a reconsideration of the identification process, particularly when it comes to changes in laws, regulations, or the legal environment.

Overall, while lawyers may not lead every aspect of the identification process, your involvement is needed to ensure a comprehensive understanding of the legal and regulatory landscape as it relates to the organization's objectives and strategies. You work collaboratively with risk management, compliance, strategy teams, and C-suite executives to provide a holistic view of the organization's opportunities, obstacles, and obligations.

Evaluating Approaches to Risk, Reward, and Compliance

Organizational leadership must regularly evaluate their current and planned approaches to addressing risk, reward, and compliance. This process involves setting analysis criteria, conducting detailed assessments of risk/reward and compliance levels, evaluating current measures' adequacy, and prioritizing improvement areas.

Lawyers, particularly those specializing in compliance or risk management, play a significant role in this analysis process. At the outset, you contribute to defining the criteria for analyzing and prioritizing opportunities, obstacles, and obligations. This includes helping establish quantitative and qualitative techniques to estimate risk, reward, and compliance levels, especially in areas related to legal and regulatory matters. To do so effectively, you must build your knowledge of metrics design and work closely with experts in this area.

In analyzing risk and reward, you provide crucial insights into the legal and regulatory aspects of opportunities and obstacles. You must help assess the likelihood and consequences of legal risks, contributing to the determination of inherent and residual risk levels based on the adequacy of current actions and controls. Your expertise is particularly valuable in evaluating legal and compliance-related risks that could impact your client organization's objectives.

When it comes to analyzing compliance, lawyers take a leading role. You assess mandatory and voluntary obligations, determining the level of compliance based on existing actions and controls. This involves thoroughly reviewing legal requirements, industry standards, and the organization's policies and procedures.

Your legal team contributes to evaluating the adequacy of current measures by assessing whether the existing levels of residual risk and compliance are acceptable from a legal and regulatory standpoint. You also help determine if additional analysis is required, particularly in areas with significant legal implications.

Lawyers should play a key role in validating the analysis results, especially those related to legal risks and compliance. You should communicate and negotiate these findings with other organizational units, ensuring that legal and compliance considerations are properly understood and integrated into the overall analysis.

When prioritizing areas for design modifications, lawyers provide crucial input on the importance and potential impact of legal and compliance issues. You should help balance these considerations against other business priorities, ensuring that efforts to address opportunities, obstacles, and obligations align with legal requirements and risk tolerances.

Throughout this analysis process, legal teams may suggest modifications to objectives or strategies based on the insights gained from the risk and compliance analysis. You must work closely with other leaders to ensure the organization's goals remain achievable within the legal and regulatory framework. Lastly, in this role, you should contribute to defining events or timescales that should trigger a reconsideration of the analysis, particularly when it comes to changes in laws, regulations, or the legal environment.

Overall, while lawyers may not lead every aspect of the analysis process, your involvement is critical in ensuring a comprehensive understanding of legal and compliance risks and your potential impact on the organization's objectives and strategies. You must work collaboratively with risk management, compliance, strategy teams, and C-suite executives to provide a holistic view of the organization's risk and compliance profile.

PLANNING FOR A MULTINATIONAL ENTITY

For a multinational business or organization, designing an aligned business plan is more complex, requiring you to consider international implications at every stage:

Providing Clear Direction

When setting the organization's direction in a multinational context, you must:

- Ensure the mission, vision, and values resonate across diverse cultural contexts while maintaining legal compliance in all jurisdictions
- Advise on how different legal systems and regulatory environments might impact strategic goals
- Help balance global consistency with necessary local adaptations in strategic planning
- Consider international stakeholders' diverse expectations and legal rights in different jurisdictions

Defining Objective-Setting Criteria

For global organizations, objective-setting criteria should:

- Incorporate compliance goals that address regulatory requirements across all relevant jurisdictions
- Consider how legal risks and opportunities vary across different international markets

- Ensure measurable indicators are meaningful and legally relevant in diverse cultural and regulatory contexts
- Account for varying legal standards and business practices in different countries when assigning accountability

Identifying Opportunities, Obstacles, and Obligations

In an international context, you must help:

- Identify cross-border opportunities and associated legal considerations
- Recognize potential obstacles arising from conflicting regulations or cultural differences across jurisdictions
- Map out obligations stemming from international treaties, foreign laws, and global industry standards
- Assess how geopolitical factors might impact the organization's legal risks and opportunities globally

Evaluating Approaches to Risk, Reward, and Compliance

For multinational corporations, this evaluation should:

- Consider how risk appetites and regulatory expectations vary across different countries and regions
- Analyze potential rewards and risks of international expansion or cross-border operations
- Ensure compliance approaches are effective across diverse legal systems and cultural contexts
- Develop strategies for managing conflicting legal or regulatory requirements in different jurisdictions

Overall, if you are working in this context, you must help create a business plan for your client organization that is globally coherent yet flexible enough to address the unique legal, regulatory, and cultural challenges of each jurisdiction where the organization operates. This requires a deep understanding of international business law, cross-cultural competence, and the ability to balance global strategic objectives with local compliance requirements.

SUMMARY: CONTRIBUTING TO A WELL-DESIGNED BUSINESS PLAN

These points summarize the most important tasks in which you apply your unique legal expertise to ensure the organization's business plan is fully aligned with its mission, vision, values, objectives, operating context, and the identified risks, rewards, and requirements:

- Advise on legal and regulatory considerations in setting organizational direction, including mission, vision, and values
- Provide input on legal implications and risks associated with strategic goals and objectives
- Identify and assess legal and regulatory risks that could impact organizational objectives
- Lead the identification and analysis of mandatory and voluntary legal obligations
- Evaluate the adequacy of current risk management and compliance measures from a legal perspective
- Validate and communicate analysis results related to legal risks and compliance to other organizational units
- Suggest modifications to objectives or strategies based on legal risk and compliance analysis
- Help define triggers for reconsidering direction, objectives, and analysis based on legal and regulatory changes
- Ensure alignment of organizational strategies with legal requirements and risk tolerances
- Collaborate with other departments to integrate legal and compliance considerations into strategic planning and risk management

Operationalizing GRC Strategies

Following the development of the aligned business plan, organizations operationalize GRC strategies by implementing a mix of proactive, detective, and responsive actions and controls that work together to create a comprehensive framework for managing organizational performance, risk, and compliance.

You can play a vital role in ensuring these actions and controls operate as intended by serving as a key advisor and taking leadership roles in specific areas. Legal involvement ensures that implemented actions and controls align with legal and regulatory requirements, support ethical business practices, and effectively manage legal risks.

For example, you can contribute significantly to policy development, compliance education, issue notification and inquiry systems design, and the formulation of response strategies. You can help ensure that controls are legally sound, that communication and education efforts effectively convey legal and compliance requirements, and that response mechanisms address issues thoroughly while protecting the organization's legal interests.

Lawyers are needed to translate legal and compliance requirements into practical, operational measures. You help bridge the gap between legal theory and business practice, ensuring that the organization's day-to-day activities align with its governance, risk management, and compliance objectives. Your expertise is particularly valuable in areas such as investigations, crisis management, and decision-making around disclosures and disciplinary actions.

Establishing a Mix of Actions and Controls

Every organization should have a mix of action and control types to address opportunities, obstacles, and obligations. This is foundational in operationalizing the organization's governance, risk management, and compliance strategies.

Lawyers, particularly those specializing in regulatory compliance or risk management, play a significant role in ensuring these actions and controls operate as intended. Your involvement spans the establishment and execution of proactive, detective, and responsive actions and controls.

You contribute to establishing proactive actions and controls by developing and reviewing policies and procedures that encourage favorable events and prevent unfavorable ones. You may lead efforts in creating compliance programs, drafting codes of conduct, and establishing guidelines for ethical business practices. Your expertise is particularly valuable in ensuring these proactive measures align with legal requirements and industry best practices.

For detective actions and controls, lawyers collaborate with those in other GRC roles to design monitoring systems that identify actual or potential legal and compliance issues. You may be involved in establishing whistleblower hotlines and employee helplines, developing internal audit procedures, and creating reporting mechanisms for potential legal violations. Your input is crucial in ensuring these detective measures are legally sound, respect privacy, and adhere to labor laws.

Lawyers also play a central role in the realm of responsive actions and controls. They are usually at the forefront of managing responses to unfavorable events, such as regulatory investigations or legal disputes. You may lead in developing and implementing corrective action plans, conducting internal investigations, and advising on disciplinary actions. Your expertise is essential in ensuring that responsive measures address the immediate issues and root causes while complying with legal requirements.

Lawyers also help ensure that actions and controls are neither under-controlling nor over-controlling from a legal perspective. Your input is valuable in stress testing actions and controls, particularly by identifying potential legal vulnerabilities or areas where controls might be circumvented.

Finally, lawyers play a key role in maintaining the audit trail by documenting changes to established actions and controls. You must ensure that decisions on discipline and control changes are properly recorded, providing a defensible position should these decisions be scrutinized in the future.

During the implementation of these controls, you work closely with other departments, such as compliance, risk management, and operations, as you provide a legal perspective on how various controls might impact the organization's risk profile and legal position. Your involvement helps ensure that the mix of actions and controls addresses business needs and aligns with legal and regulatory requirements.

Overall, while lawyers are not the sole implementers of these controls, their involvement ensures that the organization's approach to addressing opportunities, obstacles, and obligations is legally sound, compliant with regulations, and aligned with the organization's risk tolerance. You serve as a key advisor and leader in developing a robust and legally defensible system of actions and controls.

Creating and Managing Policies

Organizations establish policies to address opportunities, obstacles, and obligations and set clear expectations for conduct within the organization and its extended enterprise. Lawyers play an essential role in this element, leading or heavily contributing to drafting policies and defining how a policy is managed throughout its lifecycle.

Lawyers, particularly those specializing in ethics and compliance, often take a leading role in developing codes of conduct. They work with various stakeholders to ensure the code aligns with the organization's mission, vision, and values while meeting legal and regulatory requirements. Your legal expertise is valuable in crafting language that is both clear to employees and legally sound.

Establishing a policy framework is another area where your legal input is invaluable. You help create a structured approach for identifying, creating, approving, enforcing, and updating policies and procedures. Your understanding of legal requirements and potential risks helps ensure the framework is comprehensive and legally robust.

In a global organization, strong policy development and management are especially important. Lawyers must help create policies that are globally consistent yet locally adaptable. This might involve:

- Developing a global policy framework that sets overarching principles while allowing for necessary local variations
- Ensuring policies comply with laws and regulations across all jurisdictions where the organization operates
- Considering cultural differences in policy implementation and communication
- Addressing challenges of policy enforcement across different legal systems and cultural contexts

In developing specific policies and procedures, you work closely with other departments to draft language that addresses opportunities, obstacles, and obligations from a legal perspective. Your involvement ensures that policies are both preventative and directive, balancing the need to guide behavior and prevent legal issues.

Managing policies is an ongoing process in which you can play a significant role. You may be involved in implementing, communicating, and enforcing policies. Your expertise is applied in auditing policies to ensure they operate as intended and remain relevant in light of changing legal and regulatory landscapes.

Lawyers, especially those in leadership positions, should champion policies. You may lead training sessions, provide guidance on policy interpretation, and demonstrate the organization's commitment to following its policies. This role contributes to fostering a culture of compliance and ethical behavior. You also should help balance prescriptive and proscriptive policies, adapt policies to local cultures and legal requirements while maintaining core principles, and advise on applying policies in the extended enterprise.

Lawyers may also participate in establishing ethical decision-making guidelines. You may help create frameworks that guide employees in situations not explicitly covered by the code of conduct or other policies. Your legal and ethical training makes you well suited to develop nuanced guidelines that align with legal requirements and the organization's values. You may also play a key role in prioritizing policy training based on roles and applicability, ensuring that legal and compliance policies receive appropriate attention and resources.

While policy development and management involve many stakeholders across the organization, as a lawyer, you can serve as a central figure in this process. Your legal expertise, understanding of regulatory requirements, and ability to anticipate potential legal issues make you invaluable in creating a robust policy framework that supports the organization's governance, risk management, and compliance efforts.

Communicating and Reporting

Lawyers play a significant role in ensuring that the right information reaches the right audiences at the right time. They contribute to or oversee various aspects of organizational communication. Legal specialists in compliance and corporate governance may provide relevant input in establishing the communication framework. They help ensure that the framework for identifying, creating, approving, and updating communications aligns with legal and regulatory requirements. Your expertise in this field is valuable in determining appropriate senders, recipients, and channels for distinct types of communications, especially those related to legal and compliance matters.

Lawyers also play a central role in developing stakeholder reporting. You may be responsible for overseeing the creation of formal communications, reports, and filings required by mandatory obligations. This includes regulatory filings, shareholder communications for public companies, and reports required by contractual obligations. You ensure these communications meet legal requirements and protect the organization's interests.

For internal reporting, lawyers contribute by helping establish formal communications that enable effective governance and management. You may create board reports, management dashboards, and internal communications about legal and compliance matters. Your input helps ensure these reports provide information on risk management and compliance oversight.

For multinational organizations, communication and reporting strategies must account for:

- Varying disclosure requirements across different jurisdictions
- Cultural differences in communication styles and expectations
- Multi-language considerations in internal and external communications
- Compliance with international reporting standards as well as local requirements

You may work with a network of lawyers in the jurisdictions where your client organization operates to ensure that the appropriate legal guidance is provided.

While lawyers may not directly manage informal communications, they should provide guidance on their legal implications. You may develop policies on informal communication channels and advise on potential legal risks associated with different forms of informal communication.

Lawyers should also provide input on the legal and compliance implications of different communication channels. You may be particularly involved in establishing secure channels for sensitive communications, such as whistleblower hotlines or confidential reporting.

Lawyers regularly review and approve significant external communications to ensure they are legally sound and do not expose the organization to undue risk. You may be tasked with providing training or guidance to other employees on effective and compliant communication practices.

In addressing the risk of information overload or distortion through multiple communication layers, you may advise structuring communication processes to ensure legal and compliance information is not lost or misinterpreted as it moves through the organization.

Throughout these practices, you help ensure that communications balance transparency and protection of sensitive information. You also play a role in maintaining accurate records of communications for compliance and assurance purposes.

While communication involves many stakeholders across the organization, lawyers play a key role in ensuring that communications, especially those related to legal and compliance matters, are accurate, timely, and compliant with relevant laws and regulations. Your involvement helps mitigate legal risks associated with organizational communications and supports effective governance and risk management.

Providing Education and Training

While lawyers typically are not the primary drivers of all educational initiatives, they play a key role in certain aspects, particularly those related to legal compliance and risk management. Lawyers, especially those specializing in compliance or risk management, contribute significantly to defining the education plan. You may help identify key legal and compliance areas where education is necessary or legally required. Your input is valuable in determining the desired level of performance, risk, and compliance understanding for various organizational roles.

You must consider that in an international context, education and training programs need to:

- Address global compliance standards while incorporating local legal and cultural nuances

- Use culturally appropriate training methods and materials for different regions
- Consider language barriers and provide training in multiple languages when necessary
- Leverage technology for consistent global training delivery while allowing for local customization

Each of these requirements may present legal issues for consideration and resolution. You may work with your international network of legal advisors to ensure the right design.

When it comes to developing or acquiring content, lawyers often take a leading role in creating materials related to legal and compliance topics. You may develop or review content on topics such as anti-corruption laws, data privacy regulations, ethical decision-making, anti-discrimination and harassment, and industry-specific compliance requirements. Your expertise ensures that the content is legally accurate and aligned with current regulations.

You may serve as an instructor for legal and compliance-related training sessions. You might lead workshops on new regulations, conduct ethics training, or provide guidance on navigating legal issues. Your involvement helps ensure that employees understand the rules, the reasoning behind them, and their practical application. You also may contribute to developing tools, guidelines, or resources that employees can access at the point of need when facing legal or ethical dilemmas in their work.

You also may be involved in implementing a helpline by ensuring it meets legal requirements for anonymity and confidentiality where necessary. You may also be called upon to respond to inquiries, particularly those related to legal and ethical concerns.

Finally, you may contribute to measuring learning outcomes by helping define what constitutes an adequate understanding of legal and compliance matters. You may assist in developing assessments that gauge employees' grasp of relevant legal concepts and their ability to apply them in real-world situations. You should also play a key role in ensuring that the organization maintains proper training attendance and assessment records. This documentation can serve as evidence of the organization's "best efforts" to educate employees on legal and compliance matters, which can be determinative in regulatory investigations or legal proceedings.

While educational initiatives involve many stakeholders across the organization, lawyers play a vital role in ensuring that legal and compliance education is comprehensive, accurate, and effective. Your involvement helps create a workforce that is well informed about legal obligations and ethical standards, supporting the organization's overall governance, risk management, and compliance efforts.

Incentivizing Desired Conduct

Organizations implement incentives to encourage proactive, detective, and responsive conduct in the workforce and extended enterprise. While human resources and management are primarily responsible for designing and implementing incentive programs, lawyers play an advisory and oversight role in this element.

Lawyers contribute by ensuring that the types of conduct being incentivized align with legal and regulatory requirements. You help articulate conduct expectations that drive business performance and promote compliance and ethical behavior. Your input is valuable in developing legally sound and defensible definitions and classifications of desired conduct.

Regarding hiring and promoting based on conduct expectations, you should provide guidance on incorporating ethical and compliance considerations into job descriptions, career paths, and performance review criteria. You can help ensure these practices align with labor laws and do not inadvertently create discriminatory practices. You may also advise on the legal implications of using conduct criteria for promotions, ensuring fairness and consistency.

Lawyers review compensation, reward, and recognition programs when an organization implements economic incentives. You help ensure that these programs do not inadvertently incentivize unethical or noncompliant behavior. You may also advise on the legal implications of different incentive structures, particularly in regulated industries in which certain types of incentives may be restricted.

For noneconomic incentives, you may provide input on how to structure these programs to reinforce ethical behavior and compliance. You might also advise on the legal aspects of professional development programs or career opportunity structures to ensure they are fair and nondiscriminatory.

Lawyers help ensure that incentives balance prescriptive and proscriptive norms without creating perverse incentives that could encourage adverse conduct. You play a key role in identifying potential legal risks in incentive programs, such as those that might inadvertently encourage employees to cut corners or violate regulations to meet performance targets.

Lawyers also contribute to ensuring consistency in the application of incentives to avoid perceptions of favoritism or mistrust, which could lead to legal challenges. You may advise on the legal implications of different types of recognition and how to implement them fairly across the organization.

In the context of hiring criteria, you should provide guidance on how to structure these to attract candidates who align with the organization's ethical standards while ensuring compliance with employment laws and avoiding discriminatory practices.

As in the case of policy management and training, you must consider that an incentive structure in a multinational organization may have specific requirements, including the need to:

- Balance global consistency with local market norms and legal requirements
- Consider cultural differences in what motivates employees across different regions
- Ensure compliance with varying labor laws and regulations in different countries
- Address potential conflicts between global corporate culture and local business practices

Overall, while the design and implementation of incentive programs involve multiple stakeholders, lawyers ensure these programs are legally sound, promote ethical behavior, and align with the organization's compliance objectives. Your involvement helps create incentive structures that drive performance and reinforce the organization's commitment to integrity and compliance, supporting overall governance and risk management efforts.

Managing Issue Notification Processes and Response

Organizations must implement multiple pathways for people and systems to report progress toward objectives and the occurrence of both favorable and unfavorable events. Lawyers play a key role in ensuring that notification systems comply with legal requirements and protect the organization and its stakeholders.

In implementing pathways to capture favorable events, you may advise on how to structure these systems to protect sensitive business information while still allowing for the recognition of successes. You might also provide guidance on how to use this information in external communications without creating legal risks.

For pathways to capture unfavorable events, lawyers play a vital role. You may be involved in designing and implementing whistleblower systems and other reporting mechanisms for compliance violations or ethical concerns. You also will ensure these systems meet legal requirements, such as those mandated by Sarbanes-Oxley[3] or Dodd-Frank[4] in the US or similar laws and regulations in other jurisdictions.

In filtering and routing notifications, lawyers provide input on prioritizing and handling different types of reports, especially those involving legal or compliance issues. You may help develop protocols for escalating serious issues and ensuring that sensitive information reaches the appropriate decision-makers.

Lawyers serving multinational organizations must consider that issue notification and response systems need to:

- Comply with varying whistleblower protection laws across different jurisdictions
- Provide multiple reporting channels that are culturally appropriate and accessible across all regions
- Ensure consistent response protocols while allowing for necessary local adaptations
- Consider data privacy laws that may affect cross-border information sharing during investigations

[3] H.R. 3763–107th Congress: Sarbanes-Oxley Act of 2002.

[4] H.R. 4173–111th Congress: The Dodd-Frank Wall Street Reform and Consumer Protection Act.

Protecting notification information is an area where legal expertise is paramount. You must ensure that notification systems comply with data protection laws, maintain confidentiality where required, and protect the identities of whistleblowers. You also should advise on record-keeping practices to ensure that notification data can be used effectively in internal investigations or, if necessary, in legal proceedings.

Throughout these practices, you help ensure that notification pathways are designed to encourage internal reporting, which gives the organization more flexibility in addressing issues. You also might train management on how to handle notifications, especially those involving potential legal or ethical violations. You can play a key role in ensuring that anonymous reporting options are available where legally required or permitted, balancing the need for anonymity with the organization's ability to investigate and address reported issues.

Lawyers can even contribute to designing user-friendly notification systems that meet legal requirements. You may advise on the language used in reporting forms or hotlines to ensure that it encourages reporting without creating legal exposure for the organization.

You also should help ensure that notification systems extend to the organization's extended enterprise where appropriate, advising on how to implement reporting mechanisms for vendors, contractors, and other external stakeholders. You need to ensure that notification systems involving multiple stakeholders are legally compliant, protect both the organization and those who report issues, and effectively capture the information needed for risk management and compliance efforts. Your involvement helps create robust notification pathways that support the organization's governance, risk management, and compliance objectives while minimizing legal risks.

Discovering Favorable and Unfavorable Events

In the same way that multiple notification pathways are necessary, organizations must have multiple pathways to proactively discover information about progress toward objectives and the occurrence of both favorable and unfavorable events. Lawyers play a significant advisory and oversight role in designing and managing these pathways, particularly in legal compliance and risk management areas.

You must keep in mind that for global organizations, discovery processes should:

- Account for varying legal and cultural attitudes toward monitoring and surveillance across different countries
- Implement discovery methods that are effective and appropriate in different cultural contexts
- Ensure compliance with international data protection regulations in information gathering and analysis
- Consider potential language and cultural barriers in interpreting discovery findings

In implementing pathways to discover favorable events, you may advise how to structure these inquiry systems to gather information useful for legal and compliance purposes, such as evidence of effective controls or successful risk mitigation strategies. You might also provide guidance on using this information in external communications or regulatory reporting without creating legal risks.

Lawyers play a more significant role in pathways to discover unfavorable events. You should help design inquiry processes that can detect potential legal violations, compliance issues, or ethical concerns early. This might include advising on the types of questions to include in surveys or self-assessments or helping establish protocols for management observations and conversations that can uncover potential issues.

In establishing an approach to surveys and information requests, lawyers contribute by ensuring that these tools comply with data protection laws and respect employee privacy rights. You may also advise how to frame questions to gather the necessary information without creating unnecessary legal exposure for the organization.

When it comes to gathering information through observations and conversations, lawyers typically provide managers with training or guidelines on how to conduct these informal inquiries in a way that respects legal rights and does not create liability. You should also advise on how to document these interactions appropriately to ensure the maintenance of any legal privilege.

In this context, you analyze information and findings and identify the legal and compliance implications of the gathered data. You prioritize findings with potential legal ramifications and advise on appropriate escalation and management response routes.

Throughout these efforts, you ensure that inquiry pathways encourage open and honest feedback while protecting the organization's legal interests. You may be involved in developing protocols to separate inquiry responses from individual performance appraisals to maintain the integrity of the process. You may also advise on coordinating survey efforts throughout the organization to avoid fatigue while still gathering necessary legal and compliance information, helping balance the need for comprehensive information with the potential legal risks of over-inquiry.

Lawyers provide input on how to interpret and use information from various pathways in a legally sound manner when consolidating and reconciling it. You may advise on how to present findings to management and stakeholders in a way that accurately represents the legal and compliance landscape without creating undue alarm or complacency.

Overall, while implementing inquiry systems involves multiple stakeholders, lawyers ensure these systems are legally compliant, protect both the organization and those providing information, and effectively gather data needed for risk management and compliance efforts. Your involvement helps create robust inquiry pathways that support the organization's governance, risk management, and compliance objectives while minimizing legal risks.

Responding to Events

Many lawyers say they play a leading role in investigations, crisis management, and decision-making regarding disclosures and disciplinary actions. While this responsibility is widely recognized, the full scope of the lawyer's involvement may be too narrowly defined.

Lawyers play a leading role in correcting and recovering from unfavorable events. You advise on the legal implications of various recovery strategies, help navigate potential liabilities, and ensure recovery efforts comply with relevant laws and regulations. Your input is essential in developing action plans that address immediate issues and protect the organization's legal interests.

In an international context, event response strategies must:

- Consider potential cross-border implications of local events
- Ensure crisis response plans are adaptable to different cultural and legal environments
- Navigate varying disclosure requirements and expectations across different jurisdictions
- Coordinate responses across multiple regions while maintaining a consistent global approach

You may provide guidance on structuring legally acceptable incentives and rewards to recognize, compound, and accelerate favorable events. You might also advise on potential legal risks associated with certain types of recognition or acceleration strategies.

Lawyers usually take the lead in implementing investigations. You typically develop and oversee internal investigation processes, ensuring they are thorough, fair, and legally sound. Lawyers also maintain attorney-client privilege where appropriate, manage the legal risks associated with investigations, and advise on how to respond to external inquiries or investigations.

Lawyers are key advisors in crisis response planning and execution. You help develop crisis response plans that account for legal obligations and potential liabilities. During a crisis, you provide real-time legal advice on response strategies, help manage communication to minimize legal exposure, and ensure the organization's actions comply with relevant laws and regulations.

Lawyers also participate in after-action reviews, particularly for events with legal implications. You help identify legal and compliance-related root causes and advise on improving actions and controls to prevent future issues.

Lawyers may be involved in discipline and retraining by ensuring that disciplinary measures are consistent, fair, and compliant with employment laws. You may also advise on the legal aspects of retraining programs, particularly those addressing compliance issues.

Determining disclosures is another area in which legal expertise is critical. Lawyers advise on legal obligations for disclosure, help craft the content and timing of disclosures to minimize legal risk, and ensure that any external communications align with the organization's legal strategy.

Throughout the process, you help establish a tiered approach to responding to unfavorable events, ensuring that responses are proportionate and legally appropriate. You advise on maintaining confidentiality and protecting anonymity where required while ensuring that responses are thorough and address root causes. Lawyers play a key role in ensuring that disciplinary measures are applied consistently and objectively, maintaining the integrity of the response system and avoiding potential discrimination claims.

Lawyers provide input on strengthening legal and compliance-related controls by improving actions and controls based on response learnings. You help ensure that process changes address legal vulnerabilities identified through the response process.

Overall, while responses to favorable and unfavorable events involve multiple stakeholders across the organization, lawyers play an important role in ensuring these responses are legally sound, protect the organization's interests, and contribute to ongoing improvement in governance, risk management, and compliance efforts. Your involvement helps create a robust response capability that addresses immediate issues and strengthens the organization's overall resilience and integrity.

SUMMARY: OPERATIONALIZING THE GRC PLAN

These points capture the essential ways that lawyers contribute to operationalizing GRC strategies and ensuring legal and ethical compliance in the organization's day-to-day activities.

- Develop and review policies and procedures to ensure legal compliance and promote ethical conduct
- Design and implement compliance education programs and materials
- Advise on the legal implications of incentive structures and recognition programs
- Create and oversee whistleblower systems and other legal/ethical reporting mechanisms
- Ensure notification and inquiry systems comply with data protection and privacy laws

- Lead or advise on internal investigations and managing external inquiries
- Provide legal guidance on crisis response planning and execution
- Advise on disciplinary measures and retraining programs to ensure fairness and legal compliance
- Determine necessary disclosures and manage legal risks in external communications
- Review and improve actions and controls to address legal vulnerabilities and strengthen compliance

Improving GRC Capabilities

The GRC capability lifecycle is never ending. It includes a review and improvement loop that continuously enhances performance by monitoring the GRC actions and controls, providing assurance about priority areas, and implementing improvements. This is needed to ensure that the organization's GRC efforts remain effective, efficient, agile, and resilient in the face of changing internal and external contexts, shifts in stakeholder demands, and the occurrence of events.

Monitoring, assurance, and improvement activities work together to create a comprehensive framework for evaluating and enhancing the organization's GRC capabilities. Monitoring helps gauge the effectiveness of actions and controls on an ongoing basis. Assurance provides objective evaluations to enhance stakeholder confidence in the organization's performance, risk management, and compliance. Improvement plans focus on leveraging insights from monitoring and assurance to continuously advance the organization's capabilities.

Lawyers play a vital role throughout these steps, serving as key advisors and sometimes taking leadership roles in specific areas. Your involvement ensures that these review processes align with legal and regulatory requirements, effectively address legal risks, and support the organization's overall governance objectives.

You should significantly contribute to designing monitoring strategies, particularly for legal and compliance-related areas. You should contribute to assurance activities, leading or participating in evaluations of legal compliance and corporate governance practices. In the improvement phase, you should help identify and implement legal and compliance process enhancements based on the insights gained from monitoring and assurance activities.

Lawyers also ensure that the organization's GRC efforts remain robust and current with evolving legal and regulatory requirements. You help translate the findings from review activities into practical improvements that strengthen the organization's legal and compliance posture. Your expertise is particularly valuable in interpreting review findings and designing improvements that balance legal compliance with business objectives.

Overall, with significant input from legal professionals, organizations can continuously evaluate and enhance their GRC strategies, fostering a culture of ongoing improvement and adaptation to changing legal and regulatory landscapes.

Monitoring Operating Effectiveness and Efficiency

Ongoing and periodic review is needed to gauge the effectiveness, efficiency, agility, and resilience of GRC actions and controls. Lawyers play a significant role in designing and conducting this review, particularly in areas related to legal compliance, risk management, and governance.

In planning the monitoring approach, you contribute by ensuring that the strategy includes appropriate monitoring of legal and compliance-related actions and controls. You help identify key legal and regulatory areas that require ongoing monitoring and advise on the frequency and depth of monitoring activities needed to meet legal obligations and manage legal risks effectively.

Lawyers help identify monitoring information and determine what legal and compliance-related data should be tracked. This might include information on regulatory compliance rates, incidence of legal violations, or metrics related to the effectiveness of compliance programs. You help ensure that the monitoring information gathered sufficiently demonstrates compliance with any legal requirements.

You may be directly involved in reviewing legal and compliance-related controls when performing monitoring activities. You conduct periodic reviews of contracts, policies, and regulatory filings to ensure ongoing compliance. You may also oversee or participate in compliance audits and assessments.

Legal expertise is particularly valuable in analyzing and reporting monitoring results. Lawyers help interpret the legal implications of monitoring results, identifying areas of potential legal risk or compliance weakness. You also play a key role in recommending improvements to address any legal or compliance issues identified through monitoring activities.

Throughout these practices, you help ensure that legal and compliance-related actions and controls are effective, efficient, agile, and resilient. For example:

- Lawyers assess the effectiveness of compliance programs and legal risk management strategies by determining whether they are well-designed and operating as intended.
- For efficiency, they consider the cost-benefit ratio of legal and compliance controls, helping identify areas where resources might be better allocated.
- Regarding agility, lawyers contribute to developing systems that can quickly detect and respond to legal and compliance issues.
- For resilience, they help design backup plans and redundancies in critical legal and compliance functions.

Lawyers should know how to establish and interpret key performance indicators (KPIs), key risk indicators (KRIs), and key compliance indicators (KCIs) related to legal and regulatory matters. You must advise on appropriate targets and thresholds for these indicators, considering legal requirements and risk tolerances.

When indicators suggest potential legal or compliance issues, lawyers are involved in determining appropriate management actions. You may recommend changes to policies or practices, initiate investigations, or advise on remediation efforts. Lawyers also contribute to periodic evaluations of the GRC capability, particularly in assessing how changes in the legal and regulatory landscape might impact the organization's monitoring needs.

While monitoring activities involve multiple stakeholders across the organization, you play a key role in ensuring that these activities effectively capture and address legal and compliance risks. Your involvement helps create a robust monitoring system that supports the organization's governance, risk management, and compliance objectives while adapting to changing legal and regulatory requirements.

Evaluating and Providing Assurance About GRC Efforts

Assessing and providing assurance about priority areas in GRC actions and controls can enhance stakeholder confidence about performance levels, risk management, and compliance. Lawyers play a crucial role in this, particularly in areas related to legal compliance, risk management, and corporate governance.

Lawyers contribute significantly to formulating the assurance approach by developing strategies for assessing and monitoring legal and compliance-related areas. You can help identify actions and controls for key legal and regulatory risks that require assurance activities and advise on the appropriate frequency and depth of these assessments.

When selecting assurance assessment areas, lawyers provide valuable input on prioritizing areas based on legal and compliance risks. You help identify areas in which misunderstandings or misrepresentations could have significant legal consequences, ensuring these are included in assurance activities.

You may even take a leading role in conducting assurance assessments, particularly in legal compliance and corporate governance assessments. You may participate in internal audits of compliance programs, corporate governance practice reviews, or legal risk management strategy assessments. Your expertise is valuable in defining the desired level of assurance for legal and compliance matters and in planning and executing these assessments.

In monitoring assurance assessments undertaken by others, such as internal or external audit teams, lawyers continue to provide oversight, especially for legal and compliance-related assessments. You help ensure that follow-up actions are taken on any identified legal or compliance issues and that the assessment portfolio adequately covers the organization's legal risk landscape.

You can contribute to improving the assurance approach by incorporating lessons learned from past assessments and adapting the approach to changes in the legal and regulatory environment. You thus help ensure the assurance strategy evolves to address emerging legal risks and changing compliance requirements.

Lawyers play a key role in helping the governing authority fulfill its obligations to seek assurance about the effectiveness of the organization's legal and compliance capabilities. You can advise on what level of assurance is appropriate for different legal and compliance areas, balancing the need for confidence with resource constraints.

Lawyers also contribute to ensuring the objectivity and competence of assurance activities. You may advise on the selection of assurance providers for legal and compliance matters, helping ensure these providers have the necessary legal expertise and independence.

In the context of group or project self-assessments, you may provide guidance on how to structure these to provide meaningful assurance on legal and compliance matters while recognizing the limitations of self-assessment.

While assurance activities involve multiple stakeholders across the organization, lawyers must ensure that these activities effectively address legal and compliance risks. Your involvement helps create a robust assurance system that gives stakeholders confidence in the organization's legal and regulatory compliance, supports effective governance, and contributes to overall risk management efforts. The legal perspective in assurance activities is needed to identify potential legal vulnerabilities, ensure compliance with regulatory requirements, and maintain the integrity of the organization's governance structures.

Identifying and Implementing Beneficial Change

Reviewing information from monitoring and assurance activities is essential to identifying and implementing opportunities for improvement. While operational and management teams usually drive this, lawyers play a significant role, particularly in areas related to legal compliance, risk management, and governance.

In planning the improvement approach, lawyers contribute by helping identify and prioritize areas for improvement related to legal and compliance matters. You use insights gained from monitoring and assurance activities to recommend enhancements to policies, procedures, and controls that address legal risks or compliance weaknesses. You help ensure the improvement strategy aligns with changing legal and regulatory requirements and addresses any identified vulnerabilities.

When conducting improvement initiatives, lawyers actively implement changes related to legal and compliance areas. This might involve revising policies, enhancing compliance training programs, or strengthening legal risk management processes. You work closely with others to ensure that improvements are implemented legally and that they effectively mitigate risks.

Lawyers continue to provide oversight in monitoring improvements, particularly for initiatives related to legal and compliance matters. You help assess the effectiveness of implemented changes, ensuring that they achieve the intended legal and compliance objectives. You may also be involved in reporting on the progress and impact of these improvements to senior management and the board.

Throughout the process, you should foster a culture of continuous improvement within the legal and compliance functions, advocating for regular reviews and updates to keep pace with the evolving legal landscape. You are key in incorporating feedback loops and post-assessment activities into legal and compliance processes. You may lead or participate in root cause analyses of legal issues or compliance breaches, ensuring that lessons learned are effectively integrated into future practices.

In the context of change management, you should help ensure that improvements to legal and compliance practices are communicated effectively throughout the organization. You may assist in developing training or communication strategies to help employees understand and adapt to new legal or compliance requirements.

Lawyers also contribute to budgeting considerations for improvement activities, helping justify investments in enhancing legal and compliance capabilities by articulating the potential risks and costs of not making these improvements.

Overall, while improvement initiatives involve multiple stakeholders across the organization, lawyers are tasked with ensuring these efforts effectively enhance the organization's legal and compliance posture. Their involvement helps create a dynamic and responsive legal and compliance framework that evolves with the organization's needs and changing regulations.

The legal perspective in improvement activities is important for several reasons:

- It ensures improvements align with legal requirements and best practices.
- It prioritizes improvements for significant legal risks and compliance challenges.
- It contributes to more robust and effective legal and compliance processes over time.
- It supports the organization's overall goal of achieving Principled Performance by continuously enhancing its ability to meet legal obligations and manage legal risks.

SUMMARY: DRIVING A STRONG REVIEW AND IMPROVEMENT PROCESS

These points capture how lawyers contribute to providing review, assurance, and continuous improvement that ensures the effectiveness and efficiency of the organization's legal and compliance functions within the broader GRC framework.

- Design monitoring strategies for legal and compliance-related actions and controls
- Identify key legal and regulatory metrics for ongoing monitoring
- Participate in or oversee compliance audits and assessments
- Interpret legal implications of monitoring results and recommending improvements
- Lead or contribute to assurance activities for legal compliance and corporate governance
- Advise on appropriate levels of assurance for different legal and compliance areas
- Ensure objectivity and competence in legal and compliance assurance activities

- Identify priority areas for improvement based on legal risks and compliance challenges
- Implement enhancements to legal and compliance policies, procedures, and controls
- Provide legal oversight in the monitoring and evaluation of improvement initiatives

Conclusion

The multifaceted roles of lawyers in GRC underscore their importance in modern organizations. From understanding the operational context and designing aligned business plans to operationalizing GRC strategies and driving continuous improvement, lawyers are integral to every aspect of the GRC framework. Your unique blend of legal expertise, strategic thinking, and ethical leadership positions you as a key player in navigating the interplay of governance, risk management, and compliance.

As we have seen, these roles require lawyers to go beyond traditional legal advisory functions. You must be adept at translating legal requirements into practical business solutions, balancing risk with opportunity, and fostering a culture of compliance and ethical behavior throughout the organization. The challenges are significant, but so are the opportunities for lawyers to add value and drive organizational success.

Moving forward, lawyers in GRC must continue to adapt and evolve, embracing new technologies, developing cross-functional skills, and maintaining a holistic view of the organization's objectives and risks. By effectively fulfilling these diverse roles, lawyers can protect their organizations from legal and regulatory pitfalls and contribute significantly to strategic decision-making and long-term business success.

The following chapters delve deeper into how you can integrate your expertise across the GRC framework, navigate ethical considerations, and leverage technology to enhance your effectiveness in these roles.

Action Items

- Conduct a self-assessment of your current involvement in GRC activities, identifying areas where you're already contributing and potential gaps where you could expand your role.
- Create a "GRC map" of your organization, outlining key stakeholders, processes, and decision-making points where legal input is or should be involved.
- Develop a proposal for how you can contribute more effectively to your organization's strategic planning process, focusing on integrating legal and GRC considerations.
- Establish a regular meeting or communication channel with risk management, compliance, and internal audit colleagues to foster better cross-functional collaboration in GRC efforts.
- Design a personal action plan to broaden your business acumen, including steps like attending business strategy meetings, taking relevant courses, or seeking mentorship from business leaders in your organization.

Interview with Judit Seymour

Non-executive Director, UK Board of Scope Ratings, the European Credit Rating Agency

> ***"The ability to think beyond being 'a lawyer' or 'a risk manager' is crucial to making the career change happen."***

Switzer: Judit, you have had a very interesting career path, starting out as a barrister in private practice in the UK and then advancing in a number of corporate roles, including a stint as EMEA operational risk manager for the Royal Bank of Scotland before taking on governance positions, including your current role on the UK board of Scope Ratings, the European credit rating agency. Can you tell me a bit about that evolution and how you established your interest in risk management?

Seymour: I would love to tell you that my career progression was the result of careful planning. However, that is not how it happened. I was quite determined to be a barrister from a young age and didn't consider any other career path until after I had been in practice for over seven years and had also got married. My practice was based on small-scale corporate work, and after having invested in my development by gaining a master's in insolvency and restitution, I expected to be able to elevate my workload. This did not materialize, and I realized that as a self-employed professional, I had much less control and greater overheads than others. Additionally, I knew that eventually, I wanted to have a family but would not be able to afford maternity leave—this was not very attractive.

I did not have a clear idea of my transferable skills or career values, so I completed a careers course and was very surprised by the results, which indicated a high level of analytical thinking. It gave me the self-confidence to apply for a couple of roles in the City within financial services, and I was successful in being appointed at Moody's, the credit rating agency. My career in risk management had started. I loved the new challenge, the learning curve, and the environment. I became familiar with concepts in economics, business, and financial modeling, as well as management skills and the attractions of international business travel. I spent almost ten years at Moody's structured finance team during a period of fast growth in the European market.

The experience I gained here allowed me to move to Assured Guaranty as their chief credit officer. In this role, I built experience in a regulated environment and a much broader asset base, which deepened my understanding of risk management. As it was a small organization, I was also responsible for embedding a credit risk management framework in the UK and my first exposure to operating at the board level. At this stage of my career, I knew that I was interested in organizations that were undergoing large-scale strategic change, which needed strong engagement from the risk functions to enable success. I wanted to continue to work in environments where risk management was not just a back-office function.

This led to my role at RBS immediately after the UK government rescued it. As the head of credit within the markets team in the non-core

(*Continued*)

division (the division set up to house all the assets that were no longer core to the new business model), I found the mix of regulatory and political scrutiny, a difficult economic environment, and highly structured assets needing unwinding provided to be a very satisfying challenge. I widened my risk management experience into ERM and operational risk. In my current career path as a non-executive director, I bring all the risk experience from these organizations to bear on issues faced by various boards.

Switzer: How has your understanding of GRC evolved since you first entered the legal profession?

Seymour: Quite frankly, as a barrister, I would not have known what GRC meant, and back then, there was no Google available to help me out. My understanding of GRC has evolved grassroots up from undertaking risk analysis on a single asset to calculating risk on a given portfolio to understanding regulations and seeking to unwind complex, illiquid financial transactions, and finally by what the board is driven by and interested in. My understanding of it continues to evolve as the chair of the board at Scope Ratings UK, as the concept is dynamic. GRC means many different things, and I lean on different aspects of it, depending on the role or sector I am operating in.

Switzer: How did your legal training contribute to your various roles, and what skills, beyond legal training, do you think are most crucial for lawyers looking to specialize in risk management or participate in governance?

Seymour: My legal training and experience were crucial for my first role away from the bar, as it was my experience in UK corporate insolvency law that was relevant. Thereafter, the skills of logical thinking, detail focus, and the ability to communicate clearly, which were honed during my legal training and practice, became instrumental in progressing in my career. No doubt, the hard work ethic of the legal profession also helped!

I believe that demonstrating an eagerness to continually learn, an agile mind, professional curiosity, and broad business sense is essential to progressing away from the legal profession. In some ways, these attributes are more crucial than additional qualifications. Having said that, since leaving the bar, I have obtained various certifications in risk management as well as an MBA. Learning is never wasted.

Switzer: How do you recommend lawyers balance business and legal concerns, particularly when advising the board?

Seymour: I have to say, I no longer regard myself as a barrister or a risk manager. I am a non-executive director with a wealth of experience, including law and risk management, and I use this to support the executive directors in delivering their strategic objectives. Changing the way I think about myself is part of my career progression. The ability to think beyond being "a lawyer" or "a risk manager" is crucial to making the career change happen.

When advising a board, one must understand the audience—what is driving the board, what is the relevance of the issue you are advising on, where does it fit overall within the strategic objectives, what business deliverable it impacts on, and more. Ensure your communication style is appropriate. Have an executive summary, present your opinion in a balanced manner (both the upside and downside), quantify any risk, and leave the details in the appendices. Be pragmatic and patient and avoid legal jargon. Finally, be ready to answer off-the-wall questions!

Chapter 3
Ethical Considerations in GRC

Introduction

Lawyers often find themselves performing at the intersection of legal expertise, business strategy, and ethical responsibility. This presents a unique set of challenges that extends beyond traditional legal ethics, requiring a nuanced understanding of corporate dynamics and societal expectations.

Often, you must walk a tightrope, balancing business objectives, legal compliance, and ethical concerns. Consideration must be given to how the landscape of business ethics is evolving as transactions cross borders physically or digitally, conflicts of interest arise more frequently, and technological advances create new and challenging ethical issues.

You must navigate the delicate balance between ensuring legal compliance and recognizing the organization's resource constraints and operational realities. This might involve making recommendations about which compliance measures are absolutely necessary and which can be addressed through alternative means. For instance, when an organization cannot afford or justify the expense of the full scope of controls needed to completely ensure compliance with a particular requirement for an operation that is not material to the business, you may need to prioritize the most important controls while developing creative solutions for other areas. You may also need to advise that an objective or strategy cannot be met, given the compliance constraints, and thus should be reconsidered by the governing body or operational managers. In this case, you should be prepared to suggest modifications that allow for the overarching goals to be met, even as a specific objective or strategy must be abandoned. Try never to just say no.

You may be put into difficult ethical situations. You may be told about or find information indicating criminal, civil, or administrative wrongdoing that would lead to penalties if discovered by authorities. You may also be asked to undertake activities that directly involve you in wrongdoing. In every instance, you must be vigilant about maintaining professional independence and resist pressure that would result in a violation of professional standards or make you complicit in conduct that violates laws or regulations.

The Evolving Ethical Landscape

As lawyers' roles in GRC have transformed from purely advisory to ones that involve active participation in business decision-making, a new set of ethical considerations challenges the boundaries of traditional legal ethics.

Historically, legal ethics focused primarily on the lawyer-client relationship, with emphasis on confidentiality, loyalty, and independence. However, in the GRC context, these principles take on new dimensions. For instance, the duty of confidentiality must be balanced against the need for corporate transparency. Loyalty to the client organization may conflict with broader legal or ethical obligations to stakeholders or society. Independence can be challenged when lawyers are deeply embedded in the business operations they oversee or participate in.

There is no one right answer that applies in every situation. An ethical analysis might call for the lawyer to blow the whistle by reporting to regulators, but the legal ethics rule applied to the lawyer under client-lawyer confidentiality might prevent such a report or result in disciplinary action by the bar association if the report is filed. The right answer may depend on whether the lawyer is considered to have gained the knowledge while acting as a business operator or when being purely an advising attorney, but this may only be determined after the fact, which doesn't help the lawyer make the right decision.

As early as 1984, courts in the US have ruled that a company could not claim attorney-client privilege for communications with an in-house lawyer who was acting as a business advisor.[1] Many other cases have

[1] In re Sealed Case, 737 F.2d 94 (D.C. Cir. 1984).

followed this decision, but in a number of later cases, the courts have ruled that when a dual purpose for a communication is claimed, the burden is on the claimant to show the legal purpose was a primary reason for it.[2] This has led to lawyers sometimes consulting their own counsel to assist in making difficult and conflicting ethical decisions.

For in-house counsel with dual roles in GRC programs, these cases underscore the importance of clearly delineating when they are acting in a legal capacity versus a business capacity. When seeking to maintain privilege, it's crucial to document and be able to demonstrate that obtaining or providing legal advice was a primary purpose of the communication or work product.

Balancing Confidentiality and Transparency

One of the most significant ethical challenges faced by lawyers is balancing the duty of confidentiality with demands for transparency in modern corporate governance.

Consider a scenario in which an in-house lawyer is conducting an internal investigation into allegations of bribery in the company's overseas operations. The investigation uncovers evidence of wrongdoing by mid-level managers but also hints at the potential involvement of senior executives.

This lawyer must navigate several ethical considerations:

- Maintaining attorney-client privilege over the investigation findings
- Determining the extent and timing of disclosure to the board of directors
- Deciding whether external reporting to regulatory authorities is required or advisable
- Balancing the company's interests in remediation against potential legal and reputational risks of disclosure

---

[2] For example, In re Capital One Consumer Data Security Breach Litigation, 502 F. Supp. 3d 992 (E.D. Va. 2020); In re Premera Blue Cross Customer Data Security Breach Litigation, 296 F. Supp. 3d 1230 (D. Or. 2017); United States ex rel. Barko v. Halliburton Co., 241 F. Supp. 3d 37 (D.D.C. 2017).

This scenario illustrates the tension between maintaining confidentiality and ensuring appropriate transparency. This in-house lawyer must carefully consider how to protect legitimately privileged information while also ensuring that necessary disclosures are made to appropriate parties.

In such investigations, so-called Upjohn warnings must be provided. These warnings stem from a 1981 US Supreme Court case[3] to clarify when the lawyer represents the company, not individual employees. This distinction is vital in managing confidentiality and privilege issues in internal investigations.

Whistleblowing and Ethical Obligations

The issue of whistleblowing presents particularly difficult ethical dilemmas for lawyers in GRC roles. The case of Wadler v. Bio-Rad Laboratories, Inc.[4] provides an insightful example. Sanford Wadler, the former general counsel of Bio-Rad, was fired a few months after reporting potential Foreign Corrupt Practices Act violations to the company's audit committee. Wadler noted that the practices were endemic and that high levels of management had to know they were happening. Wadler subsequently filed a whistleblower lawsuit claiming violations of two federal laws (SOX and Dodd-Frank) and of California public policy established by prior case law, claiming he was fired as retaliation for reporting the FCPA violations to the audit committee.

This case raised several ethical questions:

- What are a lawyer's obligations when they discover potential legal violations?
- How does one balance the duty of confidentiality to the client (the company) with the ethical obligation to prevent harm?
- What protections should be afforded to lawyers who act as whistleblowers?

[3] Upjohn Co. v. United States, 449 U.S. 383 (1981).

[4] Wadler v. Bio-Rad Laboratories, Inc., 916 F.3d 1176 (9th Cir. 2019).

The Bio-Rad case highlights the need for clear protocols for internal reporting and escalation of ethical concerns. It also underscores the importance of robust whistleblower protection policies that include considerations for legal and compliance professionals.

Managing Conflicts of Interest

Conflicts of interest for lawyers working in GRC roles can be particularly nuanced and challenging to navigate. These can range from personal conflicts arising from financial interests or relationships to organizational conflicts where various parts of the business have competing interests.

Imagine a scenario in which a law firm partner with a corporate client is invited to join the board of directors. While this can provide valuable legal insight at the board level, it also creates potential conflicts. As a board member, the lawyer would have fiduciary duties to shareholders, which might sometimes conflict with the legal role of ensuring regulatory compliance and client confidentiality.

Questions to consider:

- How can the lawyer maintain independence as a legal advisor while serving on the board?
- What protocols should be in place for situations in which board decisions intersect with the legal responsibilities to the client?
- How should the lawyer handle situations in which legal advice conflicts with the board's strategic decisions?
- Can these conflicts be avoided by having a different lawyer in the law firm provide legal advice to the client in certain circumstances?
- Would these questions and answers be any different if the lawyer was an in-house general counsel?

This scenario illustrates the need for clear policies on lawyers serving in dual capacities and robust conflict-management protocols. There is no one right answer or required policy, but the topic demands attention in each organization.

Ethical Use of Technology in GRC

The rapid advancement of technology in GRC presents new ethical challenges. Consider the implementation of an AI-driven compliance monitoring system that flags potential violations based on email and communication analysis.

Ethical considerations include:

- **Privacy Concerns:** How to balance effective monitoring with employee privacy rights
- **Algorithmic Bias:** Ensuring the AI system does not unfairly target certain groups or individuals
- **Overreliance on Technology:** Maintaining appropriate human oversight and judgment in compliance processes

Imagine a scenario in which a company implements an AI system to conduct due diligence on third-party vendors. The system flags a long-standing vendor as high risk based on newly analyzed data patterns. However, the reasons for this classification are not immediately clear due to the opacity of the AI's decision-making process.

The lawyer providing risk and compliance advice and oversight must grapple with several questions:

- How do you balance the efficiency of AI-driven processes with the need for explainable and justifiable decisions?
- What level of human oversight is necessary in AI-driven compliance processes?
- How do you manage the legal and ethical implications of ending a business relationship based on AI-generated risk assessments?

This scenario highlights the need for ethical guidelines in the use of AI and other advanced technologies in GRC processes.

Cross-Border Ethical Considerations

With the increase in globalized business, GRC lawyers must navigate diverse ethical and legal landscapes. This can be particularly challenging when operating in countries with unfamiliar cultural norms or weaker rule of law.

Consider a scenario in which a US-based company is expanding operations into a country known for prominent levels of corruption. Local managers argue that certain practices, such as giving gifts to government officials, are culturally expected and necessary for business operations. An in-house attorney working in the corporate compliance group is tasked with managing this need.

The lawyer must address several issues:

- How do you design a compliance program that adheres to US anti-corruption laws while being sensitive to local cultural norms?
- What training and support are needed for local staff to navigate these ethical challenges?
- How can the appropriate response be defined if a lucrative business opportunity arises requiring engaging in practices that, while legal and accepted locally, violate the company's ethical standards?

This scenario underscores the need for nuanced, culturally aware approaches to global ethics and compliance programs.

Building an Ethical GRC Culture

Perhaps one of the most challenging tasks for lawyers working in GRC is contributing to the creation and maintenance of an ethical culture. This involves not just setting rules and policies but also fostering an atmosphere in which ethical behavior is valued and practiced.

An Ethical Decision–Making Framework

A company-wide ethical decision–making framework can be a powerful tool. It might include questions to ask as decisions are made, including:

- Is it legal?
- Does it comply with our policies and values?
- How would it look if it became public knowledge?
- Would I be comfortable if my family knew about this decision?

You can help embed ethical thinking into the organizational culture by institutionalizing such frameworks with the support of the board and senior executive team.

Maintaining and Restoring Trust

Consider a company that has recently gone through a major ethical scandal, such as a large-scale data breach that was initially covered up. The in-house counsel working with the compliance and ethics team is tasked with helping rebuild the company's ethical culture and restoring trust with stakeholders.

This process might involve:

- Conducting a thorough review of existing policies and procedures
- Implementing new training programs focused on ethical decision–making
- Establishing stronger whistleblower protections and reporting mechanisms
- Working with leadership to model ethical behavior and decision-making
- Developing transparent communication strategies to rebuild trust with customers, regulators, and the public

In another data breach scenario, a software company discovers a significant breach affecting millions of users. While there was no intent to cover up the event long term, the general counsel advised strict confidentiality during the investigation, which the internal legal team would lead. Weeks passed without public disclosure. Then, a tech blog broke the story, causing public outrage and regulatory scrutiny. The company faced lawsuits, fines, and severe reputational damage. The incident highlighted the dangers of prioritizing confidentiality over necessary transparency in crisis situations in which customers or the public may be harmed.

To put it simply, you must think beyond the immediate impulse to claim attorney-client privilege and consider how transparency can help maintain or reestablish trust in customers, regulators, and the broader community when incidents arise.

Ethics in the International Business Context

As organizations expand globally, they face a tapestry of ethical norms, cultural values, and business practices that can vary significantly from country to country. You can provide guidance on navigating these differences while maintaining a consistent ethical framework.

Ethical Relativism Versus Ethical Imperialism

Organizations that operate across different cultures often encounter the tension between ethical relativism and ethical imperialism:

- Ethical relativism is the view that ethical standards are culturally determined and that what is considered ethical can vary between societies.
- Ethical imperialism is imposing one's own ethical standards on other cultures without considering local norms.

Neither extreme is appropriate for global businesses. Instead, organizations must strive for a balanced approach that respects local customs while maintaining core ethical principles.

Variations in Ethical Standards Across Cultures

Ethical standards and expectations can vary across cultures in several key areas:

1. **Gift Giving and Hospitality:** What's considered a polite business gesture in one culture might be seen as a bribe in another.
2. **Nepotism and Relationships:** Some cultures value family connections in business, while others view this as a conflict of interest.
3. **Environmental Responsibility:** The importance placed on environmental protection can vary significantly between countries.
4. **Labor Practices:** Work hours, benefits, and employee rights expectations differ across jurisdictions.
5. **Intellectual Property:** Attitudes toward intellectual property rights and enforcement vary globally.

6. **Privacy and Data Protection:** Cultural attitudes and legal requirements regarding personal data vary widely.
7. **Corporate Governance:** Expectations for transparency, shareholder rights, and board composition differ across countries.

Navigating Ethical Dilemmas in International Contexts

Consider the scenario of a US-based company expanding into Japan, where gift giving is an important part of business culture. The ethical issues might be addressed by developing a policy that:

- Acknowledges the cultural importance of gift giving while setting clear monetary limits
- Establishes a gift registry to ensure transparency
- Educates employees on the difference between appropriate gifts and potential bribes

In another scenario, a European company begins to operate in a country with lax environmental regulations. The lawyer advising this operational unit might establish policies and procedures to ensure that the company:

- Maintains global environmental standards even where local laws are less stringent
- Collaborates with local communities and governments to promote sustainable practices
- Balances immediate costs with the long-term benefits of maintaining high environmental standards

In a third scenario, a global company must navigate conflicting data protection laws between the EU (GDPR) and other regions. The lawyer overseeing this aspect of compliance for the company advises that it:

- Implement the highest standard of data protection globally where feasible
- Clearly communicate to users how their data is handled in different jurisdictions when conflicts arise

- Work with local authorities to find compliant solutions that respect both local laws and the company's global privacy principles

Each of these scenarios demonstrates that effective pathways exist to support business objectives while maintaining strong ethical standards throughout a company's global operations.

Establishing a Balance

Navigating ethical considerations in international business contexts requires a delicate balance between respecting cultural differences and maintaining consistent ethical standards. You can contribute to this process by helping your client organization develop an ethical framework that is both globally consistent and locally sensitive.

Organizations can navigate the ethical landscape of international business by establishing core ethical principles, conducting thorough cultural due diligence, and implementing flexible yet principled policies. This approach ensures compliance with varied local standards, builds trust with diverse stakeholders, and enhances the organization's global reputation.

Ultimately, the goal is to create an ethical framework that is robust enough to withstand the pressures of diverse global operations yet flexible enough to respect and adapt to local cultural norms. This balanced approach positions ethics as a competitive advantage, allowing the organization to operate with integrity across all its global markets.

A Framework for Navigating Ethical Differences

To navigate ethical differences effectively, you should work with the organization to develop a framework that:

- **Establishes Core Ethical Principles:** Define a set of nonnegotiable ethical standards that align with the organization's values and internationally recognized ethical norms (e.g., UN Global Compact principles).
- **Conducts Cultural Due Diligence:** Before entering a new market, thoroughly research local ethical norms, business practices, and cultural values.

- **Engages Local Experts:** Collaborate with local legal and ethical experts to understand nuanced cultural perspectives on ethical issues.
- **Develops Flexible Policies:** Create ethics policies that maintain core principles while allowing for culturally sensitive implementation.
- **Provides Cross-Cultural Ethics Training:** Offer comprehensive training to help employees understand and navigate ethical differences.
- **Implements a Global Ethics Hotline:** Establish a mechanism for reporting ethical concerns that is accessible and culturally appropriate across all jurisdictions.
- **Conducts Ethical Audits:** Conduct periodic reviews of ethical practices across different regions to ensure consistency with core principles and local compliance.
- **Ensures Transparent Communication:** Clearly communicate the organization's ethical stance to all stakeholders, explaining any apparent inconsistencies in practices across regions.
- **Includes Ethical Decision-Making Guidance:** Develop a structured approach to ethical decision-making that considers both global principles and local contexts.

Conclusion

Navigating the ethical landscape presents unique challenges for lawyers, requiring you to balance traditional legal ethics with the evolving demands of modern corporate governance. From managing conflicts of interest to addressing the ethical implications of new technologies, you must remain vigilant and proactive in upholding ethical standards. Building and maintaining an ethical culture is an important task, requiring ongoing effort and leadership. As the GRC field continues to evolve, so too do the ethical considerations that lawyers face. By staying informed, embracing transparency, and consistently prioritizing ethical decision-making, you can protect your client organization and contribute to the broader goal of fostering trust and integrity in business.

Action Items

- Organize an ethics workshop for the legal team to discuss common ethical dilemmas in GRC and develop response strategies.
- Create an ethical decision–making framework tailored to your client organization's GRC challenges.
- Develop a confidentiality protocol that balances the need for transparency with legal and ethical obligations.
- Establish an ethics hotline or other reporting mechanism for GRC-related ethical concerns.
- Draft a code of ethics addressing the role of legal professionals in GRC activities.

Interview with Joe Murphy

Editor, Compliance and Ethics: Ideas & Answers

"It is important to start with the point that the practice of law and the field of compliance and ethics are very different topics. Legal training is useful but not sufficient."

Switzer: Joe, like me, you had a 20-year legal career, largely in regulatory compliance, before you took a deeper dive into the compliance business when you cofounded Integrity Interactive. Since then, you've become—shall we say—a luminary in the "C in GRC" as a leading writer and educator. Tell me a bit about that journey.

Murphy: It is a bit different for me because I didn't join a field; I actually played a role in creating it. Fresh out of law school, I worked in a law firm for a couple of years, then went in house in the old Bell System. When I joined in 1976, I immediately started doing antitrust compliance work. That was my first intro to compliance. I liked doing that and gradually realized that there were people within the company whose job was to ensure that we, as a company, did the right thing. This intrigued

(*Continued*)

me and started me thinking about the idea of internal controls in organizations to protect others from the organization's conduct.

Over time, I got involved in compliance activities in different areas: environment, regulatory, FCPA. I realized that people doing compliance work in different risk areas had quite a bit in common. While classmates I knew from law school were doing work entirely different from mine, we were still all considered "lawyers." But people doing the same work I was doing in compliance in different risk areas were not considered to be in the same field. I gradually came to the conclusion that compliance was a discrete professional field, just like law. But at the time, this wasn't recognized.

In the late 1980s, through my work in house and networking with others doing similar work, I was developing these ideas. I caught up with my college political science professor and mentor, Jay Sigler, and discussed my ideas with him. At lunch one day, he said to me, "It's time we write a book together." That led to our first book, *Interactive Corporate Compliance*, which was the first book to treat compliance as a separate subject. It was published in 1988, three years before the US sentencing guidelines, which really launched compliance as a separate field, were issued. Jay and I next wrote an article for what was then called the American Corporate Counsel Association [now the Association of Corporate Counsel]. When the sentencing commission started looking at recognizing compliance programs in corporate sentencing, the ACCA included our article in its filing with the commission.

I was speaking and writing extensively about this subject. Over my career, I have given over 100 talks and written over 200 pieces related to this topic. In 1996, I left the company and joined Kirk Jordan in a law firm that did only compliance work—the Compliance Systems Legal Group. This introduced me to entrepreneurship. In 1998, we came up with the idea of using the internet for compliance training at a time when this idea was in its infancy. We pioneered using stories, pictures, and audio rather than just reciting the law online. Back then, bandwidth was very skinny, so this was the most you could do online. This company was Integrity Interactive, which we grew until we sold it to SAI Global, which is now SAI 360.

I continue to do whatever I can to champion the field of compliance and ethics, and those who do the difficult work this profession requires.

Switzer: What skills, beyond legal training, do you think are most crucial for lawyers looking to specialize in compliance or, more broadly, GRC?

Murphy: It is important to start with the point that the practice of law and the field of compliance and ethics are very different topics. Legal training is useful but not sufficient. In fact, one could argue that skills connected with HR and management are more closely related to this field. Auditors and certified fraud examiners also have skills that may tie in more directly with the field of compliance and ethics.

Lawyers do, however, have important roles to play. Lawyers are trained to be professional and to absorb and apply new information quickly. These are important skills for a compliance professional. But there is so much more. You need to know how to manage people in organizations. You do not learn this in law school. You also need a great amount of humility so you are receptive to new learning in the compliance field. Humility, for example, is important so you can deal with all individuals in an organization, no matter what their level or title. Humility helps you to be willing to accept that all of them, no matter the title, can teach you important things.

There are two skills in particular that I recommend for everyone in this field. One is public speaking, which includes understanding how to train. This is a learned skill—you do not need to be an extrovert to master this. But you need this skill in dealing with any group, including board members, senior executives, and employees. It is something you need to study, practice, and learn. You need to know how to get and keep the attention of groups, how to reach them, how to motivate them, and how to leave a lasting impression.

The second skill is active listening. This is crucial in everything you do and at every level. If you practice this, you learn not to assume you already know what others could tell you. You learn that going out to the field, being at the "store front" or "coal face" and deep in the business, is where much of the truth about an organization can be found. But if

(*Continued*)

you don't know how to listen and already think you know everything, you will not succeed. People are ready to talk with you and help you learn what is really happening in the organization, but you have to be willing to ask and listen.

Switzer: How do you recommend lawyers balance business and legal concerns, such as a demand for transparency and a requirement or desire for confidentiality in GRC matters?

Murphy: There is an inherent challenge in our field. To be successful, the compliance team needs to be deeply involved in the operations of the business. It needs the ability to reach people with important and sometimes sensitive messages. It needs to use aggressive tools to influence large numbers of people, including those with the most power in an organization. Compliance needs to be able to reach deeply into the organization to learn what is good and what is problematic. It needs to communicate bad news up the ladder and have people learn from prior mistakes that have been made.

But in too many ways, the legal system fights us and undercuts our efforts. Surprisingly, although we are doing tough work in a tough field, as a profession, we are absolutely timid in standing up for our profession. We accept ridiculous misuse and abuse of our work. We are doing our jobs to protect others and to ensure the law reaches into the core of companies. But the legal system, rather than recognizing this, uses our work against us and our clients in a way that undercuts our ability to achieve our missions.

As professionals, we need to take steps to be effective yet do what we can to limit the risk. There are certain steps we can learn and apply. For example, we often use lawyers where privilege may be invoked. Of course, this only works in a few countries, including the US. And it can seriously limit our ability to be effective in taking action to reach everyone with the compliance message.

But while we apply Band-Aids to the situation, we are badly missing the bigger picture. We need to go at the root of the problem—that parts of the legal system unnecessarily undercut our work and that we have failed to have a strong voice where bad decisions are made. This is not to say we should be partisan on substantive legal issues. But we should be outspoken when our good work is used against our clients and us and when agencies do work that unnecessarily undercuts the value and effectiveness of our work.

This is an issue that is so important and has so much that could be done that I wrote a full law review article spelling out the problem and how we can address it. [Joseph E. Murphy, "Policies in conflict: Undermining corporate self-policing," 69 Rutgers U.L. Rev. 421 (2017), https://www.rutgerslawreview.com/wp-content/uploads/2018/01/Joseph-Murphy-Policies-In-Conflict-Undermining-Corporate-Self-Policing-69-Rutgers-UL-Rev-421-2017.pdf.]

We can deal imperfectly with the limits placed on us. But the legal system, prosecutors, and regulators need to recognize the harm they cause and work with us so we can all move effectively to prevent all forms of organizational misconduct.

Chapter 4
The Role of Lawyers in GRC Stakeholder Management

Introduction

Effective stakeholder management is a linchpin for organizational success. As a lawyer, you are a uniquely qualified leader for this critical function. Your diverse skill set and strategic positioning within organizations make you invaluable assets in navigating the multifaceted landscape of stakeholder relationships.

The spectrum of stakeholders with interest in GRC is broad and diverse, each group with its own set of interests, concerns, and influences. Internally, this includes:

- The board of directors, who oversee the organization's governance and strategic direction
- C-suite executives responsible for implementing GRC strategies
- Employees who must understand and comply with GRC policies in their daily operations

Externally, lawyers must manage relationships with:

- Regulators, who enforce compliance standards and oversee industry practices
- Shareholders with a vested interest in the organization's risk management and governance
- Business partners and suppliers whose own GRC practices can impact the organization
- The media, which shapes public perception of the organization's GRC efforts

Additionally, depending on the organization's nature, other stakeholders may include customers, local communities, industry associations, and nongovernmental organizations.

In your role as a stakeholder manager, you must navigate sometimes-conflicting interests and priorities. You must balance the need for transparency with the protection of sensitive information, align diverse stakeholder expectations with organizational capabilities and legal requirements, and maintain effective communication channels across all stakeholder groups.

You can leverage your legal skills to effectively manage these diverse stakeholder relationships as you:

- Delve into strategies for stakeholder identification and prioritization
- Apply techniques for effective communication and engagement
- Establish methods for managing stakeholder expectations and conflicts
- Use approaches to measuring and improving stakeholder satisfaction in the context of GRC initiatives

By mastering these aspects of stakeholder management, you can significantly enhance the effectiveness and success of your organization's GRC efforts.

The Lawyer's Unique Position in Stakeholder Management

The legal profession, with its emphasis on analytical thinking, clear communication, and ethical conduct, provides an excellent foundation for the nuanced task of stakeholder management. As a lawyer, you bring legal expertise to the table with a keen ability to dissect complex situations, communicate intricate concepts clearly, and navigate ethical dilemmas with finesse.

Lawyers bring a distinctive blend of skills and perspectives to stakeholder management in GRC:

- **Legal Expertise:** Deep understanding of legal and regulatory requirements
- **Analytical Skills:** Ability to analyze complex situations
- **Communication Abilities:** Clear and precise communication skills
- **Ethical Grounding:** Strong ethical foundation
- **Risk Assessment:** Skill in identifying and evaluating risks

Your skills, honed through years of legal practice, translate seamlessly into the realm of stakeholder management.

The Importance of Understanding GRC Capabilities

To truly excel in stakeholder management, you must go beyond your legal expertise. A comprehensive understanding of your client organization's GRC capabilities and efforts is paramount. This knowledge serves as the bedrock upon which effective stakeholder management is built. It lends credibility to your stakeholder interactions, ensures alignment with the overall GRC strategy, and enables proactive management of stakeholder concerns.

This comprehensive understanding is essential for several reasons:

1. **Credibility:** It allows you to speak authoritatively to stakeholders.
2. **Alignment:** It ensures stakeholder management efforts align with the overall GRC strategy.
3. **Proactive Management:** It enables anticipation of stakeholder concerns.
4. **Resource Allocation:** It helps in effectively allocating resources.
5. **Continuous Improvement:** It allows the identification of gaps in GRC processes.

You should undertake the necessary education and training in details of GRC as they are addressed in the GRC Capability Model[1] that sets the standards for GRC efforts.

[1] The GRC Capability Model published by the nonprofit think tank OCEG is available at https://www.oceg.org/standards as an open-source and free resource.

Strategies for Managing Various Stakeholders

Board of Directors

Consider your potential role in managing relationships with the board of directors. The ability to distill legal and compliance issues into clear, actionable information is crucial. Lawyers regularly prepare concise yet comprehensive reports on GRC issues for board meetings, ensuring that directors have the information they need to fulfill their oversight responsibilities effectively. Moreover, they often find themselves educating board members on emerging risks and legal developments, a task that requires not only deep knowledge but also the ability to communicate legal concepts to a non-legal audience.

C-Suite Executives

When engaging with C-suite executives, you must be able to frame GRC initiatives in terms of business objectives and value creation. This requires not just legal acumen but a deep understanding of the organization's strategic goals and operational realities. You can significantly enhance your influence and effectiveness in stakeholder management by positioning yourself as a strategic partner who can help achieve business objectives while managing risks.

Key strategies for managing relationships with C-suite executives include:

- **Business Integration:** Framing GRC initiatives in terms of business objectives
- **Risk Translation:** Translating legal risks into business terms
- **Strategic Partnership:** Positioning the legal team as strategic partners
- **Performance Metrics:** Developing KPIs that demonstrate the value of GRC initiatives

Employees

The scope of stakeholder management extends far beyond the boardroom and executive suite. Lawyers engage employees, a group often overlooked in developing GRC initiatives but essential for their success.

Here, your ability to translate legal requirements into practical, understandable guidance is valuable. You might collaborate with HR to develop engaging, role-specific training programs that educate employees on GRC matters and integrate GRC principles into the organizational culture.

External Parties

External stakeholders present another arena where lawyers' stakeholder management skills shine. Take, for instance, the delicate task of managing relationships with regulators. Lawyers often find themselves at the forefront of these interactions, establishing open lines of communication, demonstrating the organization's compliance efforts, and sometimes collaborating with regulators to shape future regulations. This requires legal expertise, diplomatic skills, and a strategic mindset.

Similarly, in public companies, lawyers often manage relationships with shareholders. They ensure clear, accurate disclosure of GRC matters in shareholder communications, articulate how GRC initiatives protect and enhance shareholder value, and often participate in shareholder engagement events to address GRC-related concerns directly.

The management of business partners and suppliers presents yet another facet of stakeholder management where your legal skills are invaluable. Developing robust due diligence processes, incorporating appropriate GRC-related clauses into contracts, and working collaboratively with key partners to align GRC practices are all areas in which legal expertise intersects with stakeholder management.

Media and Public

In an era of increased public scrutiny, lawyers often find themselves involved in managing the organization's public image regarding GRC matters. This might involve developing strategies for proactively communicating the organization's GRC efforts to the public, preparing crisis communication plans, or even positioning the organization as a thought leader in GRC through publications and speaking engagements.

Challenges and Considerations

While lawyers are well suited to these tasks, stakeholder management in GRC is not without its challenges. Balancing the often-conflicting interests of various stakeholder groups requires careful diplomacy. Translating technical legal and compliance concepts into language that resonates with different stakeholders can be a difficult task. Resource constraints often limit the time and effort that can be devoted to stakeholder management. Breaking down organizational silos to ensure effective collaboration between legal, compliance, and other departments can be an uphill battle.

Moreover, demonstrating the tangible impact of stakeholder management efforts on GRC outcomes can be challenging but essential for supporting these initiatives. You must develop metrics and narratives that clearly illustrate the value of your stakeholder management efforts in terms that resonate with different audiences within the organization.

Conclusion

Despite these challenges, the importance of effective stakeholder management in GRC cannot be overstated. As organizations navigate an increasingly diverse and ever-changing regulatory landscape and face growing expectations from various stakeholder groups, the role of lawyers in managing these relationships becomes ever more important.

You can bring a unique and valuable perspective to stakeholder management in GRC. Your legal expertise, combined with your analytical skills, communication abilities, and ethical grounding, positions you as an ideal leader in this aspect of organizational management. By leveraging your skills effectively and continually broadening your understanding of the organization's GRC capabilities, you can significantly enhance the effectiveness of GRC initiatives and elevate your role as a strategic partner in the business.

As the GRC landscape continues to evolve, so too will the demands of stakeholder management. Lawyers who embrace this challenge, continually refining their approach and adapting to new stakeholder expectations, will play a pivotal role in building more resilient, ethical, and successful organizations. In doing so, they will contribute to their organization's success and redefine the role of legal professionals in the broader business context.

Action Items

- Create a stakeholder map for your organization's GRC efforts, identifying key stakeholders and their interests, influence, and potential impact on GRC initiatives.
- Develop a communication plan tailored to different stakeholder groups, focusing on how to effectively convey GRC-related information to each group.
- Organize a cross-functional workshop to improve collaboration between legal and other departments involved in GRC activities.
- Implement a feedback mechanism to regularly gather input from stakeholders on GRC processes and initiatives.
- Design a presentation for senior management highlighting the value of legal involvement in stakeholder management within the GRC framework.

Interview with Bettye Hill

Head of Human Resources and Employment Counsel, Verra

"To build relationships, you have to be accessible, and you have to be a good thought partner, not just about matters, but about the business generally."

Switzer: We first met about 20 years ago when you were part of the team helping OCEG develop the GRC capability model in your role at Archer Daniels Midland [ADM] as the director of employment compliance. Since then, you have had experience in employment compliance in a wide range of industries and organizations of different sizes. Tell me a bit about your role at ADM, which was early in the development of GRC and even early for compliance programs.

Hill: I was hired at Archer Daniels Midland by the chief compliance officer. I was tasked with addressing all aspects of global employment compliance. This was a brand-new position, and really, it was a blank

(*Continued*)

sheet of paper for me to start from. I had to define the mission, determine how many people we needed, establish what we would be doing and how we would monitor compliance globally.

Because ADM is a big government contractor, we had specific requirements to meet, including how we would conduct investigations and maintain a hotline. My group handled any related employment complaints and administrative legal issues. In addition, we addressed policy development and training.

I developed an in-house self-audit program we utilized so that we would be ready for any audits. We would perform an internal audit in the field at different locations so that when the OFCCP, which is the Office of Federal Contract Compliance Programs, came knocking, we were ready for them.

Switzer: As you were developing that early program, were there any aspects you found particularly challenging in terms of developing the needed business processes? For example, for policies, did you and your team just write the policies and have other business managers decide how to distribute them and provide training, or did you do all of that?

Hill: Everything we did I would describe as collaborative. We tried not to be an island of our own. For things like policies, we worked very closely with both HR and the relevant managers to make sure that what we put out was understandable and made sense for their teams. We really made sure we were in lockstep with the right groups, whether it be the communications department, the human resource department, or others. Working very collaboratively across other departments is really important when you're looking at not only governance but also risk assessment needs.

Risk assessment is at the forefront of even deciding what's important to tackle because you don't want to work on things that are not going to have much of an impact. At ADM, the things that we spent the most time on were things that we felt were a higher risk for the company.

Switzer: Even before you were involved in OCEG's development of the GRC Capability Model, it seems that you had a sense and understanding of the integration needed for governance, risk, management, and compliance throughout the organizations you worked for.

Hill: Most definitely. You and I both know you can't boil the ocean. So, you have to really pick and choose, and I tend to pick around the risk factors for the company. Because you can't do everything.

Switzer: What are some of the skills that you gained as a lawyer, that you were trained on, and that you developed early in your career that really helped you the most in the role of managing risk and ensuring compliance in the employment and labor arena?

Hill: Most importantly, the communication skill of knowing how to articulate why we do what we do and be able to explain it, not in legalese terms, but so that management and employees understand it. They need to feel vested in what we're trying to do. If you fail to communicate well, they will feel that lawyers are just making us jump through hoops just for the heck of it, but we're not. There is a reason for it, so I try to make sure they understand. It may be based on lawsuits that we've seen or trends we're seeing. I always try to make sure that I'm explaining things in a way that they know that we're all in it together. We're partners, and it really is about protecting the company and mitigating as much risk as we can.

Switzer: Can you give me an example of a situation where you have really had to coordinate cross-functionally, maybe even forcing yourself into a decision-making process by reminding people there may be some legal issues here, such as regulatory compliance, so you need to involve my team?

Hill: There certainly have been times when a business segment was trying to go through a change, and they needed assistance, not only from legal but also from business operations and finance. If they were building a new facility, for example, and it was going to be outside the country, we needed a cross-sectional committee to do all the work of finding the location, vetting the people who would work there, getting all the permits, and so on, making sure that we'd be able to get what we needed to be able to start in this new location and meet the deadlines that we had created for ourselves as a business.

Sometimes, people forget to bring legal in the loop, and they get down the road before they think, oh, maybe we should ask legal if this plan is going to be okay. And sometimes they're already far down that road, and

(*Continued*)

we wish we had been able to catch it sooner. Then, it's about trying to go back and make some corrections. I think that sometimes they're moving so fast they don't even think of it. Things are just moving fast, and they need to make decisions quickly because that's how business works.

Sometimes, lawyers have gotten a reputation as being the "department of no" by slowing things down and impeding progress. But once you build strong relationships with managers and they see you are a partner, they tend to bring you in sooner. You really want your clients to come to you and ask for your input before they start going down the road, and you want them to feel like you are part of their team. To build relationships, you have to be accessible, and you have to be a good thought partner, not just about legal things, but about the business generally. You need to understand the goals and be able to contribute information that helps to achieve those goals.

Switzer: Do you have any advice that you would give a lawyer who has been working in a legal department or has been a litigator in private practice but wants to transition into more of a direct GRC role?

Hill: First of all, find your passion. What do you really enjoy? What is it that really gets you excited about what you want to do? Then, find someone who's working in that area, doing what you want to do. Connect and interact with them. See the path that they took and discuss how you could plan a similar path. Don't be shy. Networking and mentorship are, I think, really key.

Chapter 5
The Role of Lawyers in Crisis Management

Introduction

In addition to the contribution of lawyers in designing and implementing the overall GRC capability, they play a particularly important role when crises emerge swiftly and unexpectedly, threatening an organization's operations, reputation, and very existence. The spectrum of potential crises is vast and ever evolving, from cyberattacks and natural disasters to product failures and public relations nightmares. In this volatile situation, the integration of crisis management and business continuity planning into an organization's GRC framework is not just advisable—it's essential.

As a lawyer working in GRC, you play a pivotal role in this area. Your legal expertise, combined with your understanding of the organization's broader risk landscape, positions you to contribute to crisis preparedness, response, and recovery. In short, you can leverage your skills to enhance your client organization's resilience and navigate crisis management.

Understanding the Landscape

Before delving into the specific role of lawyers, it's important to understand the broader context of crisis management and business continuity planning. In the business sense, a crisis is any event that threatens to harm an organization, its stakeholders, or the general public. It's characterized by its potential for significant damage, the element of surprise, and the short decision time it often demands.

Crisis management is the process by which an organization deals with such disruptive and unexpected events. It encompasses a range of activities, from identifying potential crises before they occur to implementing strategies to deal with the crisis and its aftermath. On the other hand, business continuity planning focuses on maintaining essential functions during and after a disaster. While closely related to crisis management, it has a broader scope, aiming to ensure that business operations can continue under a wide range of circumstances.

As a GRC professional, you are already familiar with many principles underpinning effective crisis management and business continuity planning. For instance, the risk assessment techniques used in day-to-day work are directly applicable to identifying potential crises. Similarly, the compliance frameworks you might help implement contribute to preventing crises from occurring in the first place.

The Lawyer's Role in Crisis Preparedness

A lawyer's involvement in crisis preparedness begins long before any crisis occurs. One of your primary responsibilities is to conduct thorough legal risk assessments, identifying potential legal issues that could escalate into full-blown crises. This might involve analyzing the organization's contracts, reviewing its compliance with relevant regulations, or assessing its vulnerability to litigation.

Consider, for example, a technology company developing a new artificial intelligence product. The company lawyers might identify potential legal risks related to data privacy, algorithmic bias, or intellectual property infringement. By flagging these issues early, lawyers can help the organization take preventive measures, potentially averting a crisis before it begins.

Your role likely also extends to policy development. Legal professionals draft and review crisis management policies, ensuring they're practical and compliant with relevant laws and regulations. This involves working closely with other departments, such as HR, IT, and Communications, to develop comprehensive, legally sound policies.

Training and education form another part of the preparedness role. You may be tasked with developing the legal aspects of crisis management training programs or educating leadership on the legal implications of various crisis scenarios. The ability to translate legal concepts into understandable, actionable guidance is invaluable here.

Navigating the Storm: Legal Considerations in Crisis Response

When a crisis hits, the lawyer shifts from preparation to active response. In these high-pressure situations, a calm, analytical approach can be a steadying influence on the crisis management team.

The first task will likely be to assess the legal implications of the crisis. Is there potential for litigation? Are there regulatory reporting requirements that need to be met? What are the immediate steps needed to mitigate legal risks? The ability to quickly analyze these issues and provide clear, actionable advice can be key in shaping the organization's initial response.

Communication is another area where your legal input is vital. In a crisis, what an organization says—and how it says it—can have significant legal ramifications. Lawyers need to work closely with the communications team to ensure that all statements are legally sound. This involves a delicate balance: the organization needs to be transparent enough to maintain trust but careful enough to avoid creating additional legal liabilities.

You will also play a key role in managing any regulatory aspects of the crisis. This might involve ensuring compliance with reporting requirements, managing interactions with regulatory bodies, or preparing for potential investigations. Your understanding of the regulatory landscape is valuable here, as noncompliance during a crisis can compound the organization's problems.

If the crisis leads to litigation, lawyers will be at the forefront of managing this process. This involves preparing for the litigation itself and ensuring that evidence is preserved and legal holds are properly managed from the outset of the crisis.

Business Continuity: Ensuring Organizational Resilience

While crisis management often focuses on the immediate response to a disruptive event, business continuity planning takes a longer view. You have an important role to play in ensuring that your client organization can continue to function effectively, even in the face of significant disruption.

Critically, you need to identify legal functions and processes that must be maintained, even in a crisis. This might involve ensuring that contracts can still be reviewed and approved, that compliance obligations continue to be met, and that legal support remains available for key business operations.

Lawyers also need to consider succession planning from a legal perspective. What happens if key legal personnel are unavailable during a crisis? How is legal authority delegated in emergency situations? These are questions that must be addressed in business continuity planning.

Data protection and cybersecurity are other areas where legal expertise is needed. In an era when data is an organization's most valuable asset, ensuring its protection—even in crisis situations—is paramount. If you are involved in crisis management, you need to work closely with IT teams to ensure that data backup and recovery plans are technically sound and compliant with relevant data-protection laws.

Learning from the Crisis: Post-Event Considerations

Once the immediate crisis has passed, the lawyer's role evolves once again. Now, the focus is on learning from the experience and implementing changes to prevent similar crises in the future.

This often begins with a thorough legal review of the crisis and the organization's response:

- What legal issues arose that weren't anticipated?
- How effective were the organization's crisis management policies and procedures?
- Were there any compliance failures that contributed to the crisis?

Your legal analysis of these questions and answers can provide valuable insights into improving the organization's crisis preparedness.

You may also be involved in reputation management and rebuilding trust with stakeholders. This might mean developing legal strategies for addressing stakeholder concerns or advising on the legal aspects of public statements and commitments made in the wake of the crisis.

Longer term, the focus will be on enhancing the organization's overall risk management and compliance measures based on lessons learned from the crisis. This might involve updating policies, strengthening compliance programs, or implementing new legal safeguards.

Ethical Considerations: Navigating the Gray Areas

You will likely encounter ethical dilemmas that require careful navigation throughout the crisis management process. How do you balance the organization's interests with public safety concerns? When does the need for transparency outweigh legal protections? These questions don't always have clear-cut answers.

Your ethical obligations as a lawyer provide a framework for addressing these dilemmas. However, legal professionals often find themselves in situations where different ethical principles seem to conflict. In these moments, their judgment and integrity as professionals are put to the test.

Remember that the lawyer's role is to protect the organization legally and guide it toward ethical behavior. Sometimes, this might mean advising a course of action that carries more legal risk but is ultimately the right thing to do. Navigating these situations requires a deep understanding of legal and ethical principles and the ability to communicate them to decision-makers.

Leveraging Technology in Crisis Management

In today's digital age, technology plays an increasingly important role in crisis management and business continuity planning. You need to be aware of how these technologies can be leveraged effectively—and the legal implications of their use.

For instance, artificial intelligence and data analytics can be powerful tools for predicting and managing crises. They can help identify potential risks, analyze vast amounts of data quickly during a crisis, and even assist in decision-making. However, their use also raises important legal and ethical questions. How can organizations ensure that AI-driven decisions in a crisis situation are fair and nondiscriminatory? How can they manage the data privacy implications of using these technologies?

Similarly, while technology can greatly enhance an organization's ability to respond to crises, it can also be a source of crises itself. Cybersecurity breaches, for example, are an increasingly common form of crisis that organizations face. You need to be prepared to deal with the unique legal challenges these technology-related crises present.

Conclusion

Crisis management and business continuity planning are not just about responding to disasters—they are about building organizational resilience. Your legal expertise and understanding of the organization's risks and ethical obligations position you to be a key leader in crisis preparedness, response, and recovery.

By integrating crisis management into your broader GRC work, you can help your client organization survive crises and emerge from them stronger and more resilient. This requires a proactive approach, a willingness to engage with multifaceted issues, and the ability to provide clear, strategic guidance even in high-pressure situations.

Effective crisis management is an ongoing process, not a one-time event. It requires continuous learning, adaptation, and improvement. As you navigate this vital aspect of GRC, you must stay curious, remain flexible, and always be prepared to lead when the unexpected occurs.

Action Items

- Review your client organization's current crisis management plans and identify areas where legal expertise could be better integrated.
- Develop a legal risk assessment template specifically for crisis scenarios common in your industry.
- Organize a tabletop exercise simulating a GRC-related crisis involving key stakeholders from various departments.
- Create a quick reference guide outlining key legal considerations and steps to take in common crisis scenarios.
- Establish a protocol for post-crisis legal review and documentation of lessons learned.

Interview with Tom Fox

Founder and Creator, Compliance Podcast Network

"I see GRC as the next step up from legal-based compliance, with integrated GRC leading a business management approach to overall risk management."

Switzer: You've had a long career in legal private practice during which you have become a recognized leading expert in laws addressing bribery and corruption and how to build compliance programs, especially to address this issue. For the past seven years, you have also run the Compliance Podcast Network, which features more than 90 shows on a range of compliance issues. Tell me a bit about your journey and how the rise of GRC as a business management approach has played in your own career.

Fox: I was a GC of a company that had, in 2007, the largest FCPA fine ever, $27MM. Now, that number is not in the top 30 of FCPA enforcement actions. I was [among] a group of new leaders brought in after the settlement to help implement a new compliance regime. Based on that, I saw compliance as a legal response. However, as we moved into the 2010s, I began to see compliance as a business response to both corruption itself and laws preventing corruption. As I learned more and grew professionally, I began to see that more effective compliance, through integrated GRC, led to more efficient controls and greater business profitability. I see GRC as the next step up from legal-based compliance, with integrated GRC leading a business management approach to overall risk management. Now I see an integrated approach to GRC as a key component, as the driver of successful businesses to 2030 and beyond.

Switzer: What strategies have you found effective for integrating legal and GRC considerations into governance activities, such as setting business objectives and strategies?

Fox: I think we are still at the point where many organizations do not provide a seat at the table for GRC professionals to participate in the setting of long-term business objectives and strategies. That said, it is

(*Continued*)

changing for the better. As more diverse groups come into this plan, you garner a wider range of analysis, ideas, and input for long-term goals and strategy. But it all starts with a seat at the table. Additionally, the business-to-business pressure is moving more companies in this direction. As companies seek more reliable business partners, either on the sales or supply chain side they are demanding a more integrated approach around governance. There is also pressure coming from monetary funding sources such as private equity, investment funds, banks, and even insurance companies. The bottom line is that companies that have a more integrated approach are seen as better business partners.

Switzer: How do you see the balance between legal and business skills evolving for lawyers in GRC?

Fox: This has evolved for me because when I was in law school in the '80s, there was no training for business skills. Now, law schools provide a wider range of classes and skills to prepare JD candidates for a more well-rounded career. There will always be a dynamic tension between a law department and a business development type, but the analytical skills you learn as a lawyer will serve you well throughout your career. Simply put, you must understand all the roles within your company to properly serve them from the legal side of things. This means the business perspective as well as the legal perspective.

Switzer: What advice would you give to young lawyers considering a career in GRC?

Fox: GRC is one of the places to start your career. With a grounded legal education, you can layer on other skills such as compliance, governance, and risk management, which will not only make you more marketable but also provide you with a wide range of learning experiences moving forward. Be curious, always learning and always seeking out new and different assignments. Such an approach will further your immediate career as it will make you noticed within your organization, and you will also learn valuable skills that you might be able to employ down the road.

Chapter 6
Using GRC Technology

Introduction

As the complexity of GRC needs continues to grow, technology plays an increasingly essential role in supporting and streamlining GRC processes. The evolving landscape of GRC technologies and software offerings is reshaping the practice of GRC professionals, including lawyers.

In the not-too-distant past, lawyers in law firms or working at multinational corporations were often involved in manual document reviews, in-person interviews, and paper-based compliance tracking. Today, they must navigate tech-enabled operations where artificial intelligence assists in litigation discovery and contract analysis, blockchain ensures the integrity of compliance records, and advanced analytics provide real-time risk assessments. Things have changed, and you need to keep up.

Overview of GRC Technology Landscape

The GRC technology market has expanded significantly in recent years, offering a wide range of solutions to address various aspects of governance, risk management, and compliance, including legal matter management. These technologies aim to automate processes, enhance visibility, improve collaboration, and provide data-driven insights to support decision-making.

Key categories of GRC technologies include:

- Integrated GRC platforms
- Compliance management software
- Risk management solutions
- Policy management tools
- Audit management systems

- Third-party risk management platforms
- Data privacy and protection tools
- Contract lifecycle management software
- Legal matter management systems
- Regulatory change management solutions

While some organizations opt for comprehensive, integrated GRC platforms that cover multiple aspects of GRC, others choose specialized solutions for specific functions. GRC technology solutions need to be cost-effective and scalable, especially for SMEs. While large-scale integrated GRC platforms might be out of reach, there are numerous affordable options that can significantly enhance GRC efforts, including:

- Cloud-based compliance management tools with pay-as-you-go models
- Open-source risk management software that can be customized to the user's needs
- Low-code platforms for creating simple, custom GRC applications
- Collaborative tools for policy management and training
- Automated regulatory update services to stay informed about relevant changes

If you are advising SMEs, focus on solutions that offer the most critical functionalities without unnecessary complexity, ensuring that the technology investment provides tangible benefits and grows with the company.

The Future of GRC Technologies

Artificial Intelligence and Machine Learning

AI and ML are the most transformative technologies in the GRC space, offering powerful capabilities in several areas:

- **Contract Analysis:** AI-powered tools can quickly review vast numbers of contracts, identifying key clauses, potential risks, and inconsistencies.

- **Predictive Analytics:** ML algorithms can analyze historical data to predict future compliance risks or potential legal issues.
- **Natural Language Processing (NLP):** NLP technologies enable the analysis of unstructured data, such as emails or internal communications, to identify potential compliance issues or risks.

One AI contract review platform recently conducted a study in which its AI was pitted against 20 experienced lawyers in reviewing five nondisclosure agreements (NDAs). The AI completed the task in 26 seconds with 94% accuracy, while the lawyers took an average of 92 minutes with 85% accuracy. Imagine the advantages of starting with an AI review when there are thousands of documents to be evaluated. This applies to contract review and litigation discovery, compliance audit activity, and data review in risk evaluations, to name just a few use cases. But remember, your human review of AI-provided assessments or summaries is still always needed.

Consider a scenario in which a large hospital network faces the challenge of complying with new patient data privacy regulations. The compliance group, led by a member of the in-house legal department, takes a proactive approach. The team partners with IT to implement an AI-powered data management system that can automatically classify and protect sensitive patient information. They also develop a comprehensive training program for staff, using interactive online modules and simulations to ensure an understanding of the new requirements. The team establishes a compliance hotline and encourages a speak-up culture. They use data analytics to identify potential compliance risks before they become issues. As a result of these efforts, the company meets the new regulatory requirements and becomes an industry leader in data privacy practices. The proactive approach helps prevent data breaches and builds trust with patients and regulators. All this is accomplished faster and more accurately due to AI's assistance in the process.

Blockchain and Distributed Ledger Technology

Blockchain has significant applications in GRC:

- **Compliance Tracking:** Blockchain can create immutable records of compliance activities, providing a transparent and tamper-proof audit trail.

- **Smart Contracts:** These self-executing contracts with terms directly written into code can automate compliance processes and reduce the risk of human error.
- **Identity Management:** Blockchain can provide secure and decentralized identity verification systems, which are crucial for Know Your Customer (KYC) processes and privacy protection.
- **Supply Chain Traceability:** Blockchain enables transparent and immutable tracking of goods and services throughout the supply chain, which is valuable for regulatory compliance and risk management.
- **Intellectual Property Protection:** Blockchain can create tamper-proof records of intellectual property, helping establish ownership and protect against infringement.
- **Voting Systems:** Blockchain-based voting systems can enhance transparency and security in corporate governance and shareholder decisions.
- **Data Protection and GDPR Compliance:** Blockchain's inherent features can help achieve and demonstrate compliance with data protection regulations like GDPR.

Most lawyers do not realize that they need to understand, at least at a rudimentary level, how blockchain technology operates and may directly affect their areas of responsibility. You should prioritize developing a foundational understanding of blockchain technology and its applications in the legal field. This includes grasping how blockchain ensures data immutability and transparency.

As a legal professional, it's crucial for you to comprehend the potential implications of blockchain on contract law, intellectual property rights, and data privacy regulations. Additionally, you should familiarize yourself with the regulatory landscape surrounding blockchain and cryptocurrencies, as this area is rapidly evolving. Practical knowledge of how blockchain can be used for compliance tracking and audit trails is also essential, as it may become increasingly relevant in legal proceedings and due diligence processes.

In the coming years, blockchain technology is likely to significantly transform governance, risk management, and compliance practices across various industries. We can expect to see increased adoption of blockchain-based systems for real-time compliance monitoring and reporting, potentially reducing the need for traditional audits and enhancing the accuracy and efficiency of regulatory oversight. Smart contracts may revolutionize how organizations manage and enforce agreements, possibly leading to new legal challenges and opportunities. In risk management, blockchain could provide more robust and transparent systems for identity verification, supply chain tracking, and fraud prevention. As for governance, the technology might facilitate more secure and verifiable voting systems in corporate settings and enable new forms of decentralized autonomous organizations (DAOs) that could challenge traditional corporate structures. You must navigate these changes, advising your client organization on both the opportunities and potential pitfalls of blockchain implementation in GRC frameworks.

Data Analytics and Visualization

Advanced analytics tools allow GRC professionals to make sense of vast amounts of data:

- **Risk Assessment:** Data analytics can identify patterns and correlations that might indicate emerging risks.
- **Compliance Monitoring:** Analytics tools can track compliance metrics across the organization, providing real-time dashboards and alerts.
- **Reporting:** Data visualization tools can create clear, compelling reports for board members and regulators.
- **Predictive Analytics:** Machine learning algorithms can forecast potential compliance issues or risk events using historical data and trends.
- **Natural Language Processing:** NLP can analyze unstructured data from emails, contracts, and social media to identify potential compliance violations or reputational risks.
- **Process Mining:** This technique maps and analyzes business processes to identify inefficiencies, bottlenecks, and compliance gaps.

You should familiarize yourself with these data analytics and visualization tools as they become increasingly integral to legal and compliance functions. Understanding the basics of data analysis, statistical concepts, and data visualization techniques is crucial. If you work in this field, you should be able to interpret complex data visualizations, understand the limitations and potential biases in data analytics, and effectively communicate data-driven insights to stakeholders.

Furthermore, you should be aware of these tools' ethical and legal implications, particularly concerning data privacy, algorithmic bias, and the admissibility of data-driven evidence in legal proceedings. You need to understand how these tools interact with existing legal and regulatory frameworks, such as GDPR or industry-specific regulations.

Looking to the future, the use of data analytics and visualization in GRC tasks is likely to expand significantly in these ways:

- **AI-Powered Compliance:** Artificial intelligence may be used to continuously monitor and adapt compliance programs based on changing regulations and business environments.
- **Blockchain Integration:** Combining blockchain with data analytics could provide immutable audit trails and enhance the credibility of compliance reporting.
- **Augmented Reality (AR) for Risk Visualization:** AR technologies might be used to create immersive, interactive visualizations of risk landscapes and compliance metrics.
- **Sentiment Analysis:** Advanced NLP techniques could be employed to gauge public sentiment and identify potential reputational risks in real time.
- **Cross-Functional Data Integration:** GRC tools may increasingly integrate data from various business functions (finance, HR, operations) to provide a holistic view of organizational risk and compliance.
- **Automated Regulatory Reporting:** Machine-learning algorithms could automate the generation of regulatory reports, reducing manual effort and the potential for human error.

As these tools evolve, you will need to stay abreast of technological advancements and their implications for GRC practices. You may be called upon to advise on the legal aspects of implementing these technologies, ensure their use complies with relevant laws and regulations, and interpret data analytics results in legal contexts. Additionally, you may need to develop new data literacy and digital forensics skills to effectively leverage these tools in your practice.

Emerging Trends in GRC Technology

In addition to the rise of new AI-assisted GRC technologies, developments that affect the entire field of available technologies warrant continued attention and monitoring, including:

- **Robotic Process Automation (RPA):** RPA is being used to automate repetitive GRC tasks, improving efficiency and reducing human error.
- **Cloud-Native Solutions:** More GRC solutions are being built as cloud-native applications, offering greater scalability and flexibility.
- **Internet of Things (IoT):** IoT devices are being integrated into GRC systems for real-time monitoring and data collection.

International Variations and Challenges in GRC Technology Use

The adoption and implementation of GRC technology can vary significantly across different countries and regions due to various factors, including regulatory changes, technological infrastructure, cultural attitudes, and economic conditions. Lawyers involved in global GRC initiatives must help those in the organization who are deciding what technology to use understand these variations.

Examples of Factors Influencing International GRC Technology Adoption

1. **Regulatory Environment**
    - Some jurisdictions have specific requirements for GRC technologies, such as data localization laws in Russia and China.
    - The EU's emphasis on data protection (GDPR) has driven the adoption of privacy-enhancing technologies.

2. **Technological Infrastructure**
    - Developed countries often have more advanced IT infrastructure, facilitating easier adoption of GRC systems.
    - Emerging markets may rely more on mobile-based solutions due to widespread mobile device usage.
3. **Cultural Attitudes**
    - Cultures with higher trust in technology may adopt automated GRC solutions more readily.
    - Regions with a strong emphasis on personal relationships may prefer hybrid systems that balance technology with human interaction.
4. **Economic Factors**
    - Budget constraints in some regions may limit the adoption of high-end GRC technologies.
    - Cost-benefit analysis of GRC technology may vary based on local labor costs and regulatory fines.
5. **Data Sovereignty Concerns**
    - Some countries require GRC data to be stored within national borders, influencing technology choices and even decisions about areas of operation.

Regional Variations in GRC Technology Implementation

North America and Western Europe

- Generally early adopters of advanced GRC technologies
- Strong focus on integrated platforms that cover multiple GRC aspects
- High adoption of AI and machine learning in GRC processes

Asia-Pacific

- Varied adoption rates, with countries like Japan and Singapore leading in GRC tech implementation
- Growing emphasis on mobile-based GRC solutions, especially in countries like India and Indonesia
- Increasing focus on cybersecurity aspects of GRC due to rising cyber threats

Latin America

- Increasing adoption, driven by anti-corruption initiatives and data protection laws
- Growing market for cloud-based GRC solutions due to cost-effectiveness

Middle East and Africa

- Emerging GRC technology market, focusing on sectors like finance and telecommunications
- Increasing adoption of GRC solutions to meet international standards and attract foreign investment

Strategies for Global GRC Technology Implementation

1. **Modular Approach:** Implement core GRC functionalities globally, with region-specific modules to address local requirements.
2. **Cloud Versus On Premises:** Consider regulatory requirements for data storage when choosing between cloud-based and on-premises solutions.
3. **Localization:** Ensure GRC platforms support multiple languages and can adapt to local reporting requirements.
4. **Mobile Integration:** Prioritize mobile accessibility in regions with high smartphone penetration.
5. **Scalability:** Choose solutions that can scale to accommodate growth in emerging markets.
6. **Vendor Selection:** Consider vendors with a global presence and an understanding of regional compliance landscapes.

Data Privacy and Security in Cross-Border Data Transfers and International Data Governance

As organizations operate globally, managing data across borders becomes a significant GRC challenge. You must navigate and be able to advise on a broad landscape of international data protection laws and security requirements.

Key Challenges in Cross-Border Data Transfers

1. **Varying Data-Protection Laws**
   - The EU's GDPR sets strict rules for data transfers outside the EU/EEA.
   - Countries like China, Russia, and Brazil have implemented data localization requirements.
2. **Data Sovereignty**
   - Some countries assert the right to access data stored within their borders.
   - This can conflict with privacy laws in the country where the data originated.
3. **Cybersecurity Risks**
   - Cross-border data transfers can increase vulnerability to cyber attacks.
   - Different countries have varying cybersecurity standards and capabilities.
4. **Contractual Provisions**
   - International data transfers often require specific contractual safeguards.
5. **Conflict of Laws**
   - Organizations may face situations where complying with one country's laws could violate another's.

Strategies for Managing Cross-Border Data Transfers

1. **Data Mapping:** Conduct thorough data mapping to understand what data is being transferred where.
2. **Legal Basis for Transfers:** Ensure each cross-border transfer has a valid legal basis (e.g., adequacy decisions, standard contractual clauses, binding corporate rules).
3. **Data Minimization:** Transfer only necessary data to minimize risk and comply with data minimization principles.
4. **Encryption:** Implement strong encryption for data in transit and at rest.
5. **Vendor Management:** Carefully vet and monitor third-party vendors involved in data processing.
6. **Privacy Impact Assessments:** Conduct assessments for high-risk data transfers.

7. **Data Localization Strategies:** Where required, implement strategies to keep certain data within specific jurisdictions.

International Data Governance Best Practices

1. **Global Data Governance Framework:** Develop a comprehensive framework that sets global standards while allowing for local variations.
2. **Data Classification:** Implement a global data classification system to ensure consistent handling of sensitive information.
3. **Access Controls:** Establish role-based access controls that work across international operations.
4. **Incident Response Plan:** Develop a global incident response plan that accounts for varied breach notification requirements.
5. **Training and Awareness:** Provide regular training on international data protection requirements to relevant staff.
6. **Audits and Compliance Checks:** Conduct regular audits to ensure compliance with global and local data protection requirements.
7. **Privacy by Design:** Incorporate privacy considerations into the design of all new processes and technologies.
8. **Data Protection Officers:** Appoint DPOs where required and consider a global DPO network.

The international landscape of GRC technology adoption and data privacy presents both challenges and opportunities for organizations. Lawyers navigate this by ensuring that GRC technologies are implemented effectively across different regions while maintaining compliance with diverse data protection requirements. You can help your client organization turn these challenges into a competitive advantage by adopting a flexible yet robust approach to GRC technology and data governance that builds trust with stakeholders across their global operations.

Challenges and Considerations

As can be seen from the prior discussion, technologies, both old and new, offer significant benefits, but their implementation and use come with challenges, the most significant being:

- **Data Security and Privacy:** It is paramount to ensure that GRC technologies, especially cloud-based solutions, meet the organization's data security and privacy requirements.
- **Integration:** Many organizations use multiple GRC tools, and ensuring seamless integration between these systems can be challenging.
- **User Adoption:** Encouraging widespread adoption of GRC technologies across the organization requires change management efforts.
- **Customization:** While SaaS solutions offer rapid deployment, they may require customization to fully meet an organization's specific needs.
- **Keeping Pace with Technology:** The rapid evolution of GRC technologies requires ongoing learning and adaptation.
- **Ethical Considerations:** The use of AI in decision-making raises questions about transparency, accountability, and potential bias.
- **Technology Competence:** Professional associations are increasingly recognizing technology competence as part of ethical duties. GRC professionals must continually educate themselves about relevant technologies.
- **Overreliance on Technology:** While technology is a powerful tool, it should not replace professional judgment.

Addressing these challenges requires collaboration amongst a range of roles in the organization, and while you, as a lawyer, are only one member of the team, your contribution is essential in addressing each of these needs.

Strategies for Effective Technology Adoption

When assisting your client organization in developing plans to leverage technology effectively, consider the following strategies:

- **Develop a Technology Road Map:** Work with IT and business leaders to create a comprehensive plan for GRC technology adoption aligned with organizational goals.
- **Prioritize User Adoption:** Recommend investment in training and change management to ensure widespread adoption.

- **Start Small and Scale:** Begin with pilot projects to test new technologies before rolling them out organization wide.
- **Focus on Integration:** Prioritize solutions that can integrate with existing systems to create a cohesive GRC technology ecosystem.
- **Stay Informed:** Dedicate time to staying up to date with technological advancements in the GRC space.
- **Collaborate Across Disciplines:** Work closely with IT, data scientists, and business analysts to fully leverage technological capabilities.

Conclusion

The role of technology in GRC is only set to grow in the coming years. These tools are reshaping how GRC professionals approach challenges, from AI-powered analytics to blockchain-enabled compliance tracking. By embracing these technologies, GRC professionals, including lawyers in many roles, can enhance their effectiveness, provide more strategic value to their organizations, and confidently navigate the increasingly expansive regulatory landscape.

However, it is important to remember that technology is a tool, not a panacea. The most effective GRC practices always combine technological capabilities with human expertise, judgment, and ethical consideration. The most successful GRC professionals are those who can seamlessly integrate technological tools into their domain expertise, business acumen, and ethical judgment.

In this new landscape, continuous learning and adaptability are key. As a lawyer working in GRC, you must commit to ongoing education about emerging technologies, their applications, and their implications. Doing so can position you at the forefront of GRC practice, driving innovation and excellence in the field.

Action Items

- Conduct an audit of current GRC technologies used in your organization and identify areas for potential legal integration or improvement.
- Develop a plan for upskilling your legal team on key GRC technologies, including AI and blockchain applications.

- Collaborate with IT to create a data governance framework that addresses legal and compliance requirements.
- Implement a pilot project using advanced analytics for compliance monitoring or risk assessment.
- Establish a protocol for assessing the legal and ethical implications of new GRC technologies before adoption.

Chapter 7
Challenges and Opportunities

Introduction

As the role of lawyers in GRC continues to evolve and expand, legal professionals face unique challenges and opportunities, largely driven by one of the most significant shifts in the legal profession: the dual role of lawyers as legal advisors and business partners. This evolution requires lawyers to balance their traditional responsibilities with a more strategic, business-oriented approach. There are many challenges in holding these dual roles, but there are also strategies for successfully navigating their sometimes-conflicting demands.

You will benefit from taking a general assessment of your strengths and weaknesses as a lawyer working in the GRC context. By understanding these inherent qualities, you can leverage strengths and work on areas for improvement, enhancing your overall effectiveness in GRC roles. You also will need to determine how to optimize your efforts and make strategic decisions when faced with limited resources, a common scenario in many organizations.

Another necessary skill for lawyers in GRC is effective communication of legal risks. You must convey legal concepts and potential risks in a way that resonates with various stakeholders across the organization. You need to consider your role in ensuring continuous improvement in legal GRC processes. Adapting and enhancing GRC practices is key to long-term success in a rapidly changing business and regulatory environment.

Navigating Dual Roles: Legal Advisor and Business Partner

Lawyers in GRC are increasingly called upon to wear two hats: that of the traditional legal advisor and that of a strategic business partner. This dual role presents both challenges and opportunities, requiring you to balance your legal expertise with business acumen and strategic thinking.

Implementing GRC in SMEs presents additional unique challenges, primarily revolving around limited resources and the need for streamlined processes. You must be creative in developing cost-effective GRC solutions. Best practices include:

- Prioritizing risks based on the SME's specific industry and operations
- Leveraging technology to automate GRC processes where possible
- Developing multi-functional policies that address several GRC aspects simultaneously
- Training key employees to handle certain GRC responsibilities as part of their duties
- Regularly reviewing and updating GRC measures to ensure they remain relevant and effective without becoming burdensome

The key is to create a culture of compliance and risk awareness that permeates the organization without creating overly complex systems.

The Traditional Role of Legal Advisor

Historically, lawyers have been viewed primarily as technical experts in law, responsible for:

- Interpreting laws and regulations
- Ensuring compliance
- Drafting and reviewing contracts
- Managing litigation
- Protecting the organization from legal risks

This role remains important as organizations continue to need sound legal advice to navigate an ever-shifting regulatory landscape.

The Emerging Role of Business Partner

Modern organizations expect more from their legal teams. Lawyers are now called upon to:

- Contribute to strategic decision-making
- Identify business opportunities within legal constraints
- Proactively manage risks that impact business objectives
- Drive value creation through legal and compliance activities
- Align legal strategies with overall business goals

Challenges in Navigating Dual Roles

- **Maintaining Objectivity:** As you become more involved in business strategy, you risk losing the objective perspective necessary for providing unbiased legal advice.
- **Balancing Risk and Opportunity:** You must find ways to support business growth and innovation while still effectively managing legal risks.
- **Developing Business Acumen:** You may not be trained in business concepts and may struggle to understand or contribute to strategy, finance, or operations discussions.
- **Time Management:** Balancing the demands of day-to-day legal work with the need to engage in strategic business discussions can be challenging.
- **Overcoming Perceptions:** Some business leaders may still view lawyers as obstacles rather than enablers, making it difficult for them to accept you as true business partners.

Best Practices for Navigating Dual Roles

1. **Develop a Deep Understanding of the Business**
    - Immerse yourself in the organization's operations, products, and services.

- Attend business meetings and strategic planning sessions.
- Build relationships with key stakeholders across different departments.

2. **Communicate in Business Terms**
   - Translate legal concepts into business language.
   - Frame legal advice in terms of business impact and opportunities.
   - Use data and metrics to quantify legal risks and the value of legal services.
3. **Adopt a Solutions-Oriented Approach**
   - Instead of just identifying legal obstacles, propose creative solutions that achieve business objectives within legal constraints.
   - Develop a "yes, if" mindset rather than a "no, because" approach.
4. **Embrace Technology and Data**
   - Leverage legal tech tools to streamline routine legal work, freeing up time for strategic activities.
   - Use data analytics to provide insights that support business decision-making.
5. **Cultivate Business Acumen**
   - Pursue additional education in business concepts (e.g., finance, strategy, operations).
   - Seek out mentors from the business side of the organization.
   - Stay informed about industry trends and market dynamics.
6. **Maintain Ethical Standards**
   - Clearly communicate when you are switching between your legal advisor and business partner roles.
   - Establish protocols for maintaining attorney-client privilege in business discussions.
   - Be prepared to provide objective legal advice, even if it conflicts with business goals.
7. **Demonstrate Value**
   - Develop metrics that show how legal and compliance activities contribute to business success.
   - Proactively identify opportunities for the legal team to add value beyond risk mitigation.

8. **Foster Cross-Functional Collaboration**
    - Initiate and participate in cross-functional projects.
    - Act as a bridge between legal and other departments.
    - Encourage early involvement of legal in business initiatives.
9. **Practice Proactive Risk Management**
    - Anticipate potential legal issues in business strategies and propose preemptive solutions.
    - Develop and implement legal risk management frameworks that align with business objectives.
10. **Continuous Learning and Adaptation**
    - Stay updated on legal developments and their potential business impacts.
    - Seek feedback on your performance in both roles and continuously refine your approach.

By navigating these dual roles effectively, you can position yourself as an indispensable asset to your organization, contributing legal expertise, strategic insight, and business value. This approach not only enhances your professional standing but also significantly improves the overall effectiveness of the organization's GRC efforts.

Lawyers' Strengths and Weaknesses

Understanding the inherent strengths and weaknesses of lawyers in the GRC context helps maximize your effectiveness and identify areas for professional development. This self-awareness allows you to leverage your strengths while actively working to improve in areas where you, like many lawyers, may typically fall short.

Strengths

- **Analytical Skills:** Lawyers are trained to analyze situations, break down problems, and identify key issues. This skill is invaluable in navigating the intricacies of GRC.
- **Critical Thinking:** The ability to evaluate arguments, question assumptions, and make reasoned judgments is a cornerstone of legal training and essential in GRC.

- **Attention to Detail:** Lawyers are adept at spotting nuances and potential pitfalls, which is fundamental for identifying and mitigating risks.
- **Research Skills:** The capacity to find, interpret, and apply relevant information is vital in the ever-changing landscape of regulations and best practices.
- **Advocacy:** Lawyers are skilled at presenting persuasive arguments, which can be valuable when promoting GRC initiatives within an organization.
- **Ethical Reasoning:** Legal training emphasizes ethical considerations, which aligns well with the compliance aspect of GRC.
- **Contract and Document Drafting:** The ability to create clear, enforceable agreements is applied in many aspects of GRC.

Weaknesses and Areas for Improvement

- **Quantitative Skills**
  - **Weakness:** Lawyers often rely more on qualitative assessments than quantitative analysis. They may struggle with establishing measurable and auditable metrics.
  - **Improvement:** Develop skills in data analysis and statistics. Learn to create and interpret key performance indicators (KPIs) and key risk indicators (KRIs).
- **Risk Assessment Techniques**
  - **Weakness:** While lawyers are good at identifying potential legal risks, they may lack training in the comprehensive risk assessment methodologies used in GRC.
  - **Improvement:** Study and apply structured risk assessment frameworks and tools. Gain proficiency in risk mapping and quantification techniques.
- **Overreliance on Experience and Intuition**
  - **Weakness:** Lawyers rely heavily on their experience, gut feeling, and instincts, which, while valuable, may not be sufficient in GRC scenarios.
  - **Improvement:** Balance intuition with data-driven decision-making. Learn to incorporate empirical evidence and statistical analysis into risk assessments and compliance strategies.

- **Business Acumen**
  - **Weakness:** Many lawyers lack a deep understanding of business operations, finance, and strategy.
  - **Improvement:** Pursue additional education in business concepts. Actively engage with other departments to understand their functions and challenges.
- **Technology Proficiency**
  - **Weakness:** Lawyers may not be up to date with the latest GRC technologies and data management tools.
  - **Improvement:** Stay informed about GRC software solutions. Develop skills in data analytics and visualization tools.
- **Communication at Different Levels**
  - **Weakness:** While typically strong writers, lawyers may struggle to communicate legal concepts in simple terms for a non-legal audience.
  - **Improvement:** Practice translating legal jargon into plain language. Develop skills in creating visually appealing and easily understandable presentations of legal information.
- **Project Management**
  - **Weakness:** Traditional legal training does not emphasize the project management skills needed to implement GRC initiatives.
  - **Improvement:** Learn formal project management methodologies. Develop skills in planning, budgeting, and managing cross-functional teams.
- **Change Management**
  - **Weakness:** Implementing GRC initiatives requires organizational change, an area where lawyers may lack expertise.
  - **Improvement:** Study change management principles. Develop skills in stakeholder engagement and organizational psychology.
- **Strategic Thinking**
  - **Weakness:** Lawyers are trained to focus on details and specific issues, which can sometimes come at the expense of seeing the bigger picture.
  - **Improvement:** Practice systems thinking and engage in strategic planning exercises to develop a more holistic view of organizational risks and opportunities.

- **Creativity and Innovation**
  - **Weakness:** The legal profession's emphasis on precedent and risk avoidance can sometimes stifle creativity.
  - **Improvement:** Engage in brainstorming and design thinking exercises. Look for innovative solutions in other industries that could be applied to GRC challenges.
- **Emotional Intelligence**
  - **Weakness:** While usually strong in cognitive intelligence, some lawyers may struggle with emotional intelligence, which is a skill that must be applied for effective leadership and collaboration in GRC.
  - **Improvement:** Develop skills in self-awareness, empathy, and relationship management. Practice active listening and conflict resolution techniques.

By recognizing these strengths and weaknesses, you can take proactive steps to enhance your effectiveness in GRC roles. This might involve seeking out specific training, mentorship opportunities, or cross-functional experiences. Organizations should also recognize these typical strengths and weaknesses when structuring their GRC teams, ensuring a balance of skills and perspectives. The goal is to combine the unique strengths that lawyers bring to GRC with complementary skills and perspectives, creating a well-rounded approach that can navigate the complexities of modern governance, risk management, and compliance.

Managing Resource Constraints and Priorities

In GRC roles, as elsewhere, you find yourself juggling limited resources and competing priorities. This balancing act is not just about doing more with less; it is about strategically allocating resources to maximize impact and effectively manage risks while supporting organizational objectives.

The Reality of Resource Constraints

Legal departments, like other corporate functions, are frequently under pressure to control costs while expanding their scope of responsibilities. The advent of GRC has only intensified this pressure, as in-house lawyers are now expected to play a more proactive role in risk management and strategic decision-making, often without a commensurate increase in resources.

These constraints manifest in various ways:

- **Budget Limitations:** Legal departments may face restricted staffing, technology, and external counsel budgets.
- **Time Pressures:** Lawyers often manage multiple priorities with tight deadlines, which can lead to potential burnout and reduced effectiveness.
- **Staffing Challenges:** There may be a shortage of skilled professionals who understand both the legal and business aspects of GRC.
- **Technology Gaps:** Many legal departments lack access to advanced GRC technologies that could improve efficiency and effectiveness.
- **Information Overload:** The sheer volume of regulations, policies, and business information can be overwhelming, making it difficult to focus on the most critical issues.

The Importance of Strategic Prioritization

Given these constraints, effective prioritization becomes not just important but essential. As you serve in any GRC role, you must develop a strategic approach to managing your resources and priorities. This involves:

- **Aligning with Organizational Strategy:** Set priorities based on the organization's overall strategic objectives. This ensures that legal resources are focused on areas that provide the most value to the business.
- **Taking a Risk-Based Approach:** Not all risks are created equal. You must develop a keen sense of which risks pose the greatest threat to the organization and allocate resources accordingly.
- **Balancing Proactive and Reactive Work:** While responding to immediate legal issues is necessary, you must also carve out time for proactive risk management and strategic initiatives.
- **Leveraging Technology:** Embrace legal tech solutions to help automate routine tasks, freeing up time for more strategic work.

- **Collaborating and Delegating:** Collaborate with other departments and judiciously delegate tasks to help spread the workload and leverage diverse skills.

Ten Strategies for Effective Resource Management

1. **Conduct a Resource Audit:** Begin by thoroughly assessing your current resources, including personnel, budget, technology, and external partnerships. Understand how these resources are currently being utilized and identify areas of inefficiency or underutilization.
2. **Develop a Prioritization Framework:** Create a structured approach to evaluating and ranking priorities. This might involve factors such as:
    - Potential impact on the organization (financial, reputational, operational)
    - Likelihood of occurrence
    - Alignment with strategic objectives
    - Regulatory requirements and deadlines
    - Resource intensity required
3. **Implement Time Management Techniques:** Encourage the use of time management methodologies like the Eisenhower Matrix[1] (urgent vs. important) to help the legal team focus on high-impact activities.
4. **Leverage Technology Strategically:** Invest in GRC technologies that can automate routine tasks, improve risk monitoring, and enhance reporting capabilities. While there may be upfront costs, the long-term efficiency gains can be substantial.
5. **Build a Flexible Talent Pool:** To address fluctuating workloads, develop a mix of in-house expertise, external counsel relationships, and flexible staffing options (like legal consultants or temporary professionals).
6. **Foster Cross-Functional Collaboration:** Build strong relationships with other departments to share resources, information, and responsibilities. This can help distribute the workload and bring diverse perspectives to GRC challenges.

---

[1] https://sps.columbia.edu/sites/default/files/2023-08/Eisenhower%20Matrix.pdf.

7. **Implement a Triage System:** Develop a system for quickly assessing and categorizing incoming legal issues, ensuring that high-priority matters receive immediate attention while less important issues are appropriately scheduled.
8. **Regular Review and Adjustment:** Priorities and resource needs can shift rapidly. Implement a regular review process to reassess priorities and reallocate resources.
9. **Develop Clear Communication Channels:** Ensure that there are clear processes for communicating priorities and resource constraints to both the legal team and other stakeholders in the organization.
10. **Invest in Training and Development:** Prioritize the development of your team's skills in areas like project management, technology use, and business acumen. This investment can lead to significant efficiency gains over time.

Navigating Difficult Decisions

Even with the best prioritization strategies, inevitably, you face tough decisions about where to allocate limited resources. This might involve:

- Deciding to outsource certain functions to free up in-house resources for strategic priorities
- Pushing back on noncritical requests from business units to focus on higher-risk areas
- Making the case for additional resources by demonstrating the ROI of GRC activities
- Choosing to delay or scale back certain initiatives to focus on more pressing matters

In these situations, lawyers must:

- Base decisions on data and objective criteria whenever possible
- Clearly communicate the rationale behind decisions to all stakeholders
- Be prepared to adjust course if new information or changing circumstances arise
- Document decision-making processes for future reference and continuous improvement

The Role of Leadership

Managing resource constraints and priorities effectively requires strong leadership from senior lawyers and GRC professionals. This involves:

- Setting a clear vision and strategy for the legal/GRC function
- Advocating for necessary resources at the executive level
- Making tough decisions about priorities and resource allocation
- Fostering a culture of efficiency and continuous improvement
- Leading by example in time management and prioritization

By effectively managing resource constraints and priorities, you can maximize your impact and add significant value to the organization despite limitations. This strategic approach helps you manage risks more effectively and positions the legal team as a partner in achieving organizational objectives.

Effective Communication of Legal Risks

Effective communication of legal risks is a key skill you must develop. Identifying and understanding these risks are not enough; you must convey them in ways that resonate with various stakeholders, from C-suite executives to frontline employees.

The Communication Challenge

Legal risks involve nuanced issues that can be challenging to explain to non-lawyers. Moreover, different stakeholders within an organization have varying levels of legal knowledge, risk tolerance, and information needs. Your challenge is bridging this gap, translating legal concepts into language and frameworks accessible to and actionable for your audience.

Common pitfalls in communicating legal risks include:

- Overuse of legal jargon
- Failing to contextualize risks within the broader business landscape
- Overwhelming audiences with too much detail

- Not clearly articulating the potential impact on business objectives
- Focusing solely on negative outcomes without offering solutions
- Neglecting to tailor the message to different audiences

Principles of Effective Risk Communication

- **Know Your Audience:** Understand your audience's background, priorities, and information needs. A board member requires information different from that of a department manager or a frontline employee.
- **Contextualize the Risk:** Frame legal risks within the context of the organization's strategic objectives, market conditions, and competitive landscape. This helps stakeholders understand why the risk matters.
- **Use Clear, Concise Language:** Avoid legal jargon and terminology. Explain concepts in plain language that non-lawyers can easily understand.
- **Quantify Where Possible:** While not all legal risks can be precisely quantified, providing data and metrics can help make the risk more tangible. This might include potential financial impacts, likelihood of occurrence, or benchmark data from similar situations.
- **Provide a Balanced View:** While it is important to highlight potential negative outcomes, also discuss potential opportunities or positive aspects of risk management strategies.
- **Offer Solutions:** Do not just present problems; come prepared with potential solutions or mitigation strategies. This proactive approach demonstrates value and helps move the conversation forward constructively.
- **Use Visual Aids:** Charts, graphs, and other visual representations can help convey information more easily. Risk heat maps, for instance, can be particularly effective in illustrating the relative severity of different risks.
- **Encourage Dialogue:** Create opportunities for questions and discussion. This ensures understanding and helps uncover additional perspectives on the risk.

Strategies for Effective Risk Communication

To overcome communication challenges, lawyers should employ these strategies:

- **Develop a Risk Communication Framework:** Create a structured approach to risk communication that can be consistently applied across distinct types of legal risks. This might include:
  - A standard format for risk reports
  - Guidelines for translating legal concepts into business terms
  - Templates for presenting risks to different audiences
- **Tailor Your Approach to Different Stakeholders:** Develop different communication strategies for various groups within the organization:
  - **Board of Directors:** Focus on strategic-level risks, governance implications, and long-term impacts.
  - **C-Suite Executives:** Emphasize business impact, resource implications, and alignment with corporate strategy.
  - **Business Unit Leaders:** Highlight operational impacts, compliance requirements, and risk mitigation strategies relevant to their specific areas.
  - **Employees:** Focus on practical, day-to-day implications and clear guidelines for compliance.
- **Leverage Technology:** Utilize GRC software and data visualization tools to create dynamic, interactive risk reports. These can allow stakeholders to drill down into specific areas of concern and see real-time updates on risk status.
- **Develop Risk Narratives:** Create compelling narratives around key risks that go beyond dry facts and figures. Use real-world examples, case studies, or hypothetical scenarios to illustrate the potential impact of risks.
- **Establish Regular Risk Communication Channels:** Implement routine risk reporting mechanisms, such as monthly dashboards, quarterly risk reviews, or annual risk assessments. This helps keep legal risks on the radar of key stakeholders.
- **Collaborate with Other Functions:** Work closely with other departments, such as finance, operations, and IT, to develop a holistic

view of risks. This cross-functional approach can provide valuable context and credibility to your risk communications.

- **Provide Training and Resources:** Offer training sessions or workshops to help key stakeholders understand legal risks and risk management concepts better. Develop resources like risk glossaries or quick reference guides that can support ongoing risk awareness.
- **Seek Feedback and Iterate:** Regularly solicit feedback on your risk communications. Are they clear? Actionable? Relevant? Use this input to continually refine your approach.

Navigating Sensitive Risk Communications

Sometimes, you have to communicate particularly sensitive or high-stakes legal risks. In these situations:

- **Consider Confidentiality:** Be mindful of attorney-client privilege and the need to protect sensitive information. Develop protocols for sharing information on a need-to-know basis.
- **Manage Timing and Delivery:** Consider the timing and method of communication carefully for significant risks. Sometimes, face-to-face discussions are more appropriate than written reports.
- **Prepare for Different Scenarios:** Anticipate potential questions or reactions and prepare appropriate responses.
- **Follow Up:** After communicating a significant risk, follow up to ensure the message was understood and to provide updates as the situation evolves.

The Role of Emotional Intelligence

Effective risk communication is not just about conveying information; it is also about managing emotions and building trust. You should develop your own emotional intelligence to:

- **Read the Room:** Pick up on nonverbal cues and adjust your communication style accordingly.
- **Show Empathy:** Acknowledge the challenges and pressures faced by your audience.

- **Build Credibility:** Consistently provide accurate, timely, and valuable risk insights to establish yourself as a trusted advisor.
- **Manage Your Own Emotions:** Stay calm and composed, especially when communicating high-stakes risks.

You can significantly enhance your value in any GRC role by mastering the art of effective risk communication. Clear, impactful communication of legal risks enables better decision-making, fosters a strong risk culture, and contributes to the organization's success in navigating legal and regulatory landscapes.

Continuous Improvement in Legal GRC Processes

The pursuit of excellence is never ending in the dynamic GRC landscape. Lawyers help drive continuous improvement in GRC processes, ensuring that the organization keeps pace with changing regulatory and business landscapes and proactively enhances its risk management and compliance capabilities.

The Imperative for Continuous Improvement

GRC processes must evolve continuously for several reasons. The regulatory landscape is in constant flux, with new laws and regulations emerging regularly. Emerging risks from new technologies, business models, and global events require adaptable processes. GRC processes must adapt to new structures and strategic objectives as organizations grow or transform. Technological advancements offer opportunities to enhance efficiency and effectiveness, while lessons learned from past experiences provide valuable insights for improvement.

The Lawyer's Role in Driving Improvement

Lawyers are uniquely positioned to drive continuous improvement in GRC processes due to their legal expertise, analytical skills, and understanding of the organization's risk profile. You might conduct regular process reviews that identify gaps, inefficiencies, and areas for improvement. This involves assessing internal processes and benchmarking against industry best practices and regulatory expectations.

Proactive regulatory monitoring is another key aspect of the lawyer's role. By staying abreast of regulatory changes and emerging legal trends, you can proactively assess the impact on current GRC processes and propose necessary adjustments. This forward-thinking approach helps organizations stay ahead of regulatory curves rather than scrambling to catch up.

Lawyers also play a role in leveraging technology for GRC improvement. You should explore and advocate for the adoption of advanced GRC technologies, collaborating with IT to implement tools that enhance risk monitoring, compliance tracking, and reporting capabilities.

Strategies for Implementing Continuous Improvement

To effectively drive continuous improvement, you can employ several strategies:

- Establish a formal improvement process, such as the Plan-Do-Check-Act cycle.
- Develop a long-term improvement road map aligned with organizational goals.
- Encourage innovation through channels for team members to suggest improvements.
- Leverage external expertise through consultations and industry forums.
- Implement agile methodologies for rapid iterations and adjustments.

Cross-functional collaboration is essential in these efforts. You should engage with other departments to gain diverse perspectives, facilitate knowledge sharing, and develop integrated improvement initiatives. This collaborative approach ensures that GRC improvements consider the broader organizational context and impacts.

Overcoming Challenges

Driving continuous improvement in GRC processes is not without challenges. You face resistance to change, as employees may be comfortable with existing processes. Resource constraints can pose significant hurdles, as improvement initiatives require time and financial investment. The complexity of GRC processes, with their interconnected nature, can make improvements challenging to implement without causing unintended consequences elsewhere in the system.

Balancing improvement initiatives with business-as-usual activities can be a delicate juggling act. It is important to allocate dedicated time and resources for improvement while ensuring that day-to-day GRC activities do not suffer. Measuring the success of these improvements can also be challenging, requiring the development of clear metrics and KPIs to track the effectiveness of enhancements.

The Path Forward

Despite these challenges, the benefits of continuous improvement in GRC processes are substantial. By championing these efforts, you can significantly enhance the value you bring to your client organization. This proactive approach strengthens the organization's risk management and compliance capabilities and positions you and the overall legal team as key drivers of organizational excellence and innovation in GRC.

As the GRC landscape continues to evolve, lawyers who excel in driving continuous improvement find themselves at the forefront of organizational strategy and decision-making. By bridging gaps between departments, facilitating shared understanding, and driving cohesive GRC initiatives, you elevate your impact far beyond traditional legal boundaries, becoming an indispensable partner in your client organization's success.

APPLYING GRC TO THE LEGAL FUNCTION OR LAW FIRM

While lawyers focus on implementing GRC processes for their client organization, turning the lens inward is also important. Applying GRC principles to the legal department or law firm can yield significant benefits in efficiency, risk management, and overall performance. These include:

- **Governance in Legal Operations:** Establish clear decision-making processes, roles, and responsibilities. This includes defining reporting structures, creating committees for key areas (e.g., ethics, technology adoption), and ensuring transparency in operations.
- **Risk Management for Legal:** Identify and assess risks specific to legal operations, such as:
    - Malpractice or professional liability
    - Conflicts of interest
    - Data security and client confidentiality
    - Resource allocation and workload management
    - Regulatory compliance for the legal profession
- Develop strategies to mitigate these risks, such as implementing robust conflict-checking systems, regular training programs, and standardized matter management processes.
- **Compliance for Legal Professionals:** Ensure adherence to professional ethics rules, data protection regulations, and industry-specific compliance requirements. This might involve:
    - Regular ethics training and updates
    - Implementing client intake procedures that address anti–money laundering regulations
    - Establishing protocols for maintaining attorney-client privilege
- **Technology and Data Management:** Leverage legal tech solutions:
    - Case management systems for better governance and risk tracking
    - E-billing software to ensure compliance with client billing guidelines
    - Data analytics for performance monitoring and resource allocation
- **Continuous Improvement:** Regularly assess the effectiveness of the legal department's own GRC processes. Encourage feedback from team members and implement a system for continuous learning and adaptation.

By applying GRC principles to their operations, legal departments and law firms can enhance their performance and gain valuable insights that inform their guidance to the client organization.

Conclusion

The role of lawyers in GRC is fraught with challenges but also ripe with opportunities for those who can effectively navigate this landscape. The evolving dual role of legal advisor and business partner, the need to leverage strengths while addressing weaknesses, the constant pressure of resource constraints, the importance of effective risk communication, and the imperative for continuous improvement all contribute to making GRC a demanding yet rewarding field for legal professionals.

By embracing a dual role, you can position yourself as an invaluable strategic partner for your client organization. By recognizing and working on your strengths and weaknesses, you will continually enhance your effectiveness in GRC roles. You can maximize your impact through strategic prioritization and resource management, even with resource constraints. By mastering the art of communicating legal risks effectively, you will ensure that your insights drive informed decision-making across the organization.

As the GRC field continues to evolve, so too do its challenges and best practices. The key to success lies in remaining adaptable, continuously learning, and always striving for excellence. Lawyers who successfully implement these best practices overcome the challenges inherent in GRC and position themselves as leaders in their organizations, driving value, managing risks effectively, and ensuring robust compliance.

A lawyer's journey in GRC is one of continuous growth and adaptation. By embracing this journey and leveraging the recommended strategies, you can transform challenges into opportunities and help create more resilient, ethical, and successful organizations.

Action Items

- Conduct a skills assessment of yourself or your legal team to identify strengths and areas for improvement in GRC-related competencies.

- Develop a resource allocation model for your legal department or firm that prioritizes GRC activities alongside other legal work.
- Implement a continuous improvement process for your legal GRC activities, including regular reviews and feedback mechanisms.
- Establish key performance indicators (KPIs) for measuring the effectiveness of legal contributions to GRC efforts.

Interview with Jonathan Strassberg

US Attorney at Law and Solicitor of England and Wales at True Course Ltd

"Be aware that although the context of international practice may be wide, the needs are local, unique, and sometimes obscured or not readily apparent."

Switzer: Jonathan, you are both a US commercial law attorney and an English solicitor. While you attended a US law school and started your legal career in a US law firm, you've been based in Europe and advising companies on the regulatory ins and outs of operating in the US market for quite a few years. Can you tell us about that career journey and how you got into international advisory work?

Strassberg: My move to international advisory work was, funnily enough, circuitous and not really planned when I moved to the UK in 2007. A few years before, I had taken a partial sabbatical from law to run a family property development business. After George W. Bush was reelected and the signs of economic fallout from the approaching mortgage crisis were becoming evident, I sold my properties, took a family vote, and moved to the UK, where we had a few family connections but little else.

During that first year of settling in, I noticed that, while I truly enjoyed our adopted home, it felt uncomfortable living in a country where I wasn't a lawyer. I had inadvertently stripped myself of my most valuable professional asset and a large aspect of my identity. So, I enrolled

(*Continued*)

in a program of England's Solicitor's Regulation Authority, designed to allow lawyers from foreign jurisdictions to become admitted to practice as English solicitors. At the time, it was called the Qualified Lawyers Transition Test. It's now called the Solicitor's Qualifying Examination. Happily, because American common law originates in many respects from that of England, the test was in significant measure a rehash of all I had learned in the first year of law school.

I became an English solicitor in 2009, set about investigating the opportunities for a dual-qualified lawyer, and quickly discovered a large gap in the UK market: While there were plenty of US lawyers in the UK, most all were working for large firms to serve the needs of multinational corporations. However, SMEs wishing to trade in America were left out in the cold, priced out by the very expensive advice available from large firms. This dearth of professional guidance applied not only to the US legal landscape but also to matters of cross-border tax, insurance, banking, HR advice, and other commercial and regulatory areas. My networking, therefore, became a two-pronged effort—to connect with SMEs needing US legal services and also to become familiar with the several other cross-border professionals available to assist those SMEs with the balance of their US business plans.

It's no exaggeration to say that upon arriving in the UK, the only people I knew were my immediate family and a few relatives. Professional or business contacts being nonexistent, I needed to build a network from the ground up. My research brought me to an organization called the British-American Business Council, with offices located in major cities throughout the UK. Of all the offices, the one in Birmingham seemed most aligned with my needs and aspirations. It had a very active event calendar, loads of local SMEs in lots of sectors wishing to trade with the US, a team of government advisors welcoming to new talent, and, importantly, it wasn't nearly as frenetic and competitive as London.

My first client was a travel app company, and the second was a chemicals manufacturer. During the first couple of years, the practice grew by inches until I was offered an associate position with an outstanding regional law firm in the southeast of England, heading up the American arm of their fledgling international commercial law practice. A steady wage allowed me to plow all my efforts into growing the practice, and in 2018, I went off on my own again. My practice, as they say in the UK, went from strength to strength, and I'm now something of a fixture in the UK's international legal sector, at least with regard to SMEs.

Switzer: What do you find most rewarding about your current practice? And what is most challenging?

Strassberg: Most rewarding, unquestionably, is being able to practice the profession I love in the manner and style that fits my aspirations, temperament, and ethics. I'm a generalist by nature and a commercial lawyer by preference. I have a practice that allows me to be confronted by diverse needs in a great variety of commercial enterprises. Each new experience requires new learning and a fresh approach.

Most challenging: Understanding that my practice, being transactional in nature, requires a constant stream of new clients and new matters. I, therefore, need to maintain a portfolio of clientele from diverse industries, as I never know when one or more sectors might slow. This is where accountants really have it over lawyers: Every new accountancy client is like an annuity, whereas each new law client may or may not be a one-off transaction.

Switzer: What skills did you need to develop beyond those you learned in law school to advise on risk and compliance issues for companies seeking to expand into the US market?

Strassberg: Well, law schools teach plenty about the law but not loads about the practice of law. That's got to be learned on the job. Like any profession, much depends upon your ability to communicate with clients and other non-lawyers in terms with which they can relate. People are more likely to trust what they can understand in common, intuitive terms. If you can explain your solutions in terms people can easily relate to and show specifically how those solutions solve their problems, you've placed yourself above the mass of your competitors.

Next is finding areas in service delivery where you can innovate. The more you can provide truly useful, innovative solutions, the more you eliminate competition. Legal judgment is, by definition, risk averse. But many lawyers, especially in the UK and Europe, confuse innovation and risk and thereby miss opportunities to grow their practice and service their clients.

(*Continued*)

Switzer: What advice would you give other attorneys, whether US trained or otherwise, who want to get into an international practice advising on risk and compliance issues for global operations?

Strassberg: Every country and every industry sector has a different perspective on international commerce for the simple reason that every country and sector has different needs, weaknesses, strengths, and experiences in relation to international commerce. Be aware that although the context of international practice may be wide, the needs are local, unique, and sometimes obscured or not readily apparent. For these reasons, my first bit of advice is to approach any such effort with a completely open mind, free of assumptions or preconceived notions.

One of the most formative books of my young adulthood was *Zen Mind, Beginner's Mind* by Shunryū Suzuki. A line from the prologue sums up the idea of beginner's mind: "It does not mean a closed mind, but actually an empty mind and a ready mind. If your mind is empty, it is always ready for anything; it is open to everything. In the beginner's mind, there are many possibilities; in the expert's mind, there are few." I took this approach in building my practice and refreshed it with each new project.

Chapter 8
Future Trends in GRC and the Evolving Role of Lawyers

Introduction

As we look toward the future of GRC, it is clear that the outlook is rapidly evolving. Technological advancements, shifting regulations, and changing business models are reshaping how organizations approach GRC. In this dynamic context, lawyers in GRC are also transforming, moving beyond traditional legal advisory roles to be strategic partners in navigating GRC challenges and achieving business objectives.

As GRC evolves, its impact on SMEs is significant, albeit different from that of larger enterprises. Future trends likely to affect SMEs include:

- Increased regulatory focus on smaller businesses, particularly in data protection and cybersecurity
- Growing expectations from larger partners and customers regarding GRC standards in their supply chains
- The emergence of more accessible, AI-driven GRC tools tailored for smaller organizations
- Greater emphasis on sustainability and climate factors, even for smaller companies

Whether you work with SMEs or larger organizations, you must help your clients stay ahead of these trends, finding ways to implement emerging best practices in GRC without overwhelming their organization. This may involve greater collaboration with industry associations, leveraging shared resources, and advocating for proportionate regulatory approaches.

Technological Revolution in GRC

One of the most significant trends shaping the future of GRC is the rapid advancement of technology. Artificial intelligence (AI) and machine learning (ML) are at the forefront of this revolution, offering unprecedented capabilities in risk assessment, compliance monitoring, and decision-making support. These tools continue to evolve.

AI and ML in GRC

These capabilities offer significant support to lawyers working in GRC, including:

- **Automated Compliance Monitoring and Reporting:** AI systems can continuously monitor vast amounts of data, identifying potential compliance issues in real time.
- **Predictive Risk Analytics:** ML algorithms can analyze historical data to predict future risks, allowing for proactive risk management.
- **Natural Language Processing:** AI can rapidly review and analyze contracts and regulatory documents, improving efficiency and accuracy.
- **AI-Assisted Decision-Making:** AI systems can provide data-driven insights to support decision-making in regulatory environments.

To advance as a GRC advisor, you must become comfortable and skillful in using these tools.

AI Ethics in GRC

Using AI in GRC raises new ethical considerations, including:

- **Bias and Fairness:** AI systems may inadvertently perpetuate or amplify biases present in training data. Lawyers must ensure that AI-driven GRC processes are fair and nondiscriminatory.
- **Transparency and Explainability:** As AI systems become more complex, ensuring transparency in decision-making processes becomes challenging. Lawyers need to address the "black box" problem in AI-driven compliance and risk management.

- **Accountability:** Determining responsibility when AI systems make errors or unethical decisions is a significant legal challenge.
- **Privacy and Data Protection:** The use of AI involves processing copious amounts of personal data, raising privacy concerns that lawyers must address.

As a GRC advisor, you need to develop expertise in AI ethics and work closely with technologists to develop governance frameworks for AI use. This may involve creating AI ethics committees, developing AI use policies, and ensuring compliance with emerging AI regulations.

Blockchain and GRC

Blockchain technology is poised to revolutionize GRC practices due to its inherent transparency, immutability, and decentralization characteristics. Key areas of impact include:

- **Supply Chain Transparency and Compliance:** Blockchain can provide an immutable record of supply chain transactions, enhancing traceability and compliance.
- **Audit Trails and Recordkeeping:** The technology offers tamper-proof recordkeeping, simplifying audit processes.
- **Smart Contracts for Automated Compliance:** Self-executing contracts can automate compliance processes, reducing human error.
- **Secure Sharing of Sensitive Compliance Data:** Blockchain can facilitate secure, transparent sharing of compliance information across organizations.

To be an effective legal advisor, you must understand both blockchain technology's technical aspects and legal implications, including data protection, contract law, and regulatory compliance in a blockchain environment.

The Shifting Regulatory Landscape

The regulatory environment is increasingly complex and globalized. There is a clear trend toward more stringent regulations in areas such as climate change/sustainability and data privacy.

Climate Change Regulations

Climate change is driving significant regulatory changes that affect GRC practices:

- **Mandatory Climate Risk Disclosure:** Many jurisdictions are implementing or considering mandatory climate risk disclosure requirements. Lawyers must help organizations navigate these reporting obligations.
- **Carbon-Pricing Mechanisms:** As more regions implement carbon taxes or cap-and-trade systems, lawyers help organizations understand and comply with these mechanisms.
- **Green Finance Regulations:** The growth of green bonds and sustainable finance is leading to new regulations. Lawyers play a key role in ensuring compliance and preventing greenwashing.
- **Climate Litigation:** Lawyers help organizations manage this emerging risk as climate-related lawsuits increase.

You must develop environmental law knowledge and a degree of climate science expertise to effectively advise on climate-related GRC issues.

Data Privacy and Protection

The trend toward stricter data protection regulations (e.g., GDPR, CCPA) is likely to continue:

- **Global Data Protection Standards:** Lawyers navigate an expanding global privacy landscape as more countries implement data protection laws.
- **Data Localization Requirements:** More countries are implementing data localization laws, requiring careful management of cross-border data flows.
- **AI and Data Protection:** The use of AI in data processing raises new privacy challenges that lawyers must address.

You must develop a holistic understanding of these issues and others that arise to effectively advise on emerging regulatory areas.

Evolving Corporate Governance Models

Corporate governance models are evolving in response to changing societal expectations and regulatory pressures:

- **Stakeholder Capitalism:** In some countries, there is a shift from shareholder primacy to stakeholder capitalism, in which companies are expected to create value for all stakeholders. This shift has significant implications for corporate governance and risk management.
- **Board Diversity:** There is an increasing focus on board diversity, including gender, racial, and cognitive diversity. Lawyers advise on compliance with evolving board diversity requirements and best practices.
- **Technology Governance:** As technology becomes more central to business operations, boards are increasingly required to oversee technology-related risks and opportunities. Lawyers help develop frameworks for effective technology governance.
- **Climate Governance:** Boards are increasingly expected to oversee climate-related risks and opportunities. Lawyers advise on integrating climate considerations into governance structures.
- **Long-Term Value Creation:** There is a growing emphasis on long-term value creation over short-term profits. This shift requires innovative approaches to performance metrics, executive compensation, and risk management.

You can play a key role in helping your client organization adapt its governance structures to these evolving models, balancing compliance with strategic flexibility.

The Evolving Role of Lawyers

In light of these trends, the role of lawyers in GRC is evolving significantly. Key aspects of this evolution include being:

- **Tech-Savvy Advisors:** Lawyers need to understand emerging technologies like AI and blockchain to provide effective GRC advice.

- **Ethical Leaders:** As organizations navigate ethical challenges in areas like AI and climate change, lawyers contribute to upholding ethical standards.
- **Interdisciplinary Collaborators:** Effective GRC requires collaboration across disciplines. Lawyers must work closely with data scientists, climate experts, and other specialists.
- **Strategic Risk Managers:** Lawyers help organizations navigate interconnected risks, from climate change to cybersecurity.
- **Governance Innovators:** Lawyers help design and implement new AI governance models that balance compliance, ethics, and strategic flexibility.
- **Sustainability Champions:** As sustainability becomes central to business strategy, lawyers play a key role in integrating sustainability considerations into GRC practices.

Conclusion

The future of GRC promises to be dynamic and challenging, shaped by technological advancements, regulatory changes, and evolving business models. For lawyers working in this field, these trends present exciting opportunities to expand their roles and make significant contributions to their client organizations' success.

To thrive in this evolving landscape, you must embrace continuous learning, develop new skills, and adopt a more strategic, integrated approach to GRC. Those who can successfully navigate these changes will find themselves at the forefront of their organizations' efforts to manage risks, ensure compliance, and drive sustainable growth.

The intersection of law, technology, business strategy, and sustainability in GRC will become increasingly complex in the coming years. Lawyers who effectively operate at this intersection are well-positioned to lead their organizations into the future and help shape a more resilient, ethical, and successful business landscape.

Action Items

- Create a strategy for staying informed about emerging GRC trends, including setting up news alerts and joining relevant professional associations.

- Develop a multiyear plan for evolving your own or your legal team's role in GRC, aligned with anticipated industry and regulatory changes.
- Establish a cross-functional working group to address the implications of AI and other emerging technologies on your organization's GRC practices.
- Develop a framework for assessing and adapting to new regulations in your client organization's industry, with a focus on agile compliance strategies.

Interview with Scott Mitchell

Founder, CEO, and Chair of OCEG

"Being able to take complex compliance data and turn it into visuals and insights that business leaders can actually use—that's what makes you a strategic partner rather than just the person who says 'no' to everything."

Switzer: Scott, while you aren't a lawyer yourself, as the founder of OCEG you have worked with many over the past 20+ years in developing and refining the GRC Capability Model. How did you become interested in developing the model and the concept of GRC?

Mitchell: While attending university in the 1980s, I worked as an accountant with the Small Business Administration. This led to an internship with Arthur Andersen and later a full-time job with Accenture, where I was a technologist and management consultant in the financial services industry. In 1997, during the first dot-com boom, I started a software company that built business simulators for financial services companies. These simulators were "business games" that allowed new MBA graduates to navigate the complexities of risk management in a risk-free environment. After I sold that software company, I started investing in other startups.

I've been involved in risk management and internal controls throughout my professional career. But it was after I started investing in other

(*Continued*)

startups that my interest in GRC really peaked. You see, in the early 2000s, when Enron, WorldCom, and other organizations were detonating the public markets, I had similar issues in my venture portfolio—not similar in size (my average investment was less than $1MM) but similar in character.

Unfortunately, I and others like me discovered that corporate governance, risk management, and compliance issues can impact companies of all shapes and sizes. These issues were not exotic "big company only" issues. They affected large and small companies, as well as for-profit, nonprofit, and governmental organizations. It didn't take long for a group of us to come together to find a way to make all of this easier and more effective.

That was back in 2002. If you told me back then that we'd still be working on this 20-plus years later, I'd call you crazy. But here we are, and the GRC movement is only getting bigger.

Switzer: When we first started work on the capability model, we noticed that lawyers supporting clients in regulatory compliance typically didn't have much experience in business processes. For example, they might write policies but have no role in or understanding of the policy management process. They might write that policy without considering the specific business operations that would need to apply it and what challenges might arise. What do you think lawyers supporting regulatory compliance must know beyond the law to be effective?

Mitchell: I think that certainly was true back then and, thankfully, less true now. That said, it is still true that lawyers do not typically get academic training or practical experience with business strategy and design. This is problematic because most of the matters surrounding GRC are solved with proactive business strategy and design.

What I've found really interesting is that law school offers a fantastic foundation in legal analysis, but when you step into a GRC role, there's this whole other skill set that becomes incredibly valuable. I'm talking about things like process mapping—being able to visualize how a business operates and where compliance controls need to fit in. It's not just about spotting legal risks anymore; it's about understanding how to build better business processes from the ground up.

One thing that really opened my eyes was learning that lawyers typically don't think about stakeholder journey mapping. Instead of just handing down legal requirements, you're actually tracking how different departments experience and interact with risk or compliance programs. And let me tell you, having some knowledge of data analytics is also a game-changer. Being able to take complex data and turn it into visuals and insights that business leaders can actually use—that's what makes you a strategic partner rather than just the person who says "no" to everything. Plus, understanding change management is crucial. Because let's face it, implementing new compliance programs isn't just about the rules—it's about getting people on board and making sure these changes actually stick. When you combine these business skills with legal expertise, that's when you can really start designing compliance programs that work with the business, not against it.

Switzer: You often refer to GRC professionals as Protectors, a term that resonates with lawyers. Can you elaborate on why the Protector point of view is valuable and how lawyers who embrace it can better serve their organizational clients?

Mitchell: One of the biggest misconceptions about being a strong Protector is that this is somehow about playing defense versus playing offense, so to speak. However, a strong Protector needs to know how to be both and do both. What I mean is that a strong Protector, in an organizational sense, is someone who knows how to simultaneously produce and preserve value. We call this the Protector mindset.

Lawyers can use this Protector mindset to serve their clients both proactively and reactively. The Protector mindset represents an evolution beyond the traditional defensive legal posture that many lawyers are trained to adopt. It recognizes that true protection isn't just about building legal walls or minimizing risk exposure (the defensive play), but also about enabling sustainable growth and innovation while maintaining appropriate guardrails (the offensive play).

Consider a lawyer advising on a new digital transformation initiative. A purely defensive approach might focus on identifying all potential legal risks and creating restrictive policies to avoid them. However, a lawyer operating with the Protector mindset would work proactively

(*Continued*)

with business teams to design compliant processes that enable innovation rather than stifle it. They would help identify opportunities where strong governance can actually create competitive advantages and contribute to building resilient frameworks that allow the business to move quickly while staying within risk boundaries.

The key insight here is that preservation (defense) and production (offense) of value aren't mutually exclusive—they're actually synergistic when approached correctly. A strong Protector understands that their role isn't to just say "no" to risky initiatives but rather to help find ways to say "yes, and here's how we can do it safely and effectively." This mindset transforms the lawyer's role from being perceived as a business blocker to being recognized as a strategic enabler who helps the organization thrive while keeping it safe.

Switzer: We're seeing lawyers engage in a range of GRC roles more often now, beyond regulatory compliance, but they often lack the education or training to be effective business leaders. What can the OCEG certification suite provide them to ensure success?

Mitchell: The OCEG certification suite uniquely addresses the breadth of GRC and goes deep into each discipline. Lawyers already working in aspects of GRC can study the bodies of knowledge and earn each of the OCEG GRC certifications to enhance their understanding of how legal needs are supported through business processes.

For lawyers building a career in various aspects of GRC, OCEG certifications offer significant value by bridging the gap between traditional legal expertise and the integrated operational approach that modern GRC demands. The certifications, particularly the GRC Professional (GRCP) and GRC Audit (GRCA) credentials, demonstrate a lawyer's commitment to understanding how legal requirements intersect with business processes, risk management, and compliance frameworks. This expertise is increasingly vital as organizations seek legal counsel who can not only interpret regulations but also help implement practical, technology-enabled GRC programs.

The more specialized certifications, such as the Integrated Compliance and Ethics: Professional (ICEP), Integrated Risk Management Professional (IRMP), Integrated AI Professional (IAIP), and the Integrated

Data Privacy Professional (IDPP), prepare lawyers to work closely with leadership in these key roles or become leaders themselves. Overall, the OCEG certifications signal to employers and clients that a lawyer possesses both the technical knowledge and the strategic mindset needed to guide organizations through complex regulatory landscapes while creating business value.

Chapter 9
Building a GRC-Focused Legal Career

Introduction

The field of GRC offers a dynamic and rewarding career path for lawyers. As organizations across all sectors increasingly recognize the critical importance of effective GRC practices, the demand for legal professionals with specialized GRC expertise continues to grow. This chapter provides a comprehensive road map for lawyers looking to build a successful career in GRC, covering diverse career paths in both private and public sectors, essential skills, professional development opportunities, and key certifications.

Private Sector Career Paths in GRC for Lawyers

GRC offers diverse career opportunities for legal professionals across various industries. Let's explore some common paths.

In-House GRC Counsel

Working within an organization to develop and implement GRC strategies. This role involves:

- Developing and overseeing compliance programs
- Managing legal risks across the organization
- Advising on corporate governance matters
- Collaborating with other departments to integrate GRC practices

Possible Career Progression: Junior Counsel → Senior Counsel → Associate General Counsel → General Counsel

GRC Outside Counsel or Consultant

Advising multiple organizations on GRC best practices and implementation. This path allows for exposure to various industries and GRC challenges. Responsibilities might include:

- Conducting GRC assessments for clients
- Designing and implementing GRC frameworks
- Providing expert advice on regulatory compliance
- Helping organizations navigate risk landscapes

Possible Career Progression: Associate or Consultant → Principal → Partner

Chief Compliance Officer

Focusing specifically on ensuring organizational compliance with laws and regulations. This role involves:

- Developing and maintaining compliance policies and procedures
- Designing compliance training and awareness programs
- Managing internal investigations
- Reporting to senior management and the board on compliance matters

Possible Career Progression: Compliance Analyst → Compliance Manager → Chief Compliance Officer

Chief Risk Officer

Overseeing the organization's risk management efforts. This role requires a broad understanding of various risk types, including legal, operational, and strategic risks. Responsibilities include:

- Developing and implementing risk management frameworks
- Identifying and assessing organizational risks and assisting in risk management plans
- Reporting on risk status to the board and senior management
- Cultivating a risk-aware culture within the organization

Possible Career Progression: Risk Analyst → Risk Manager → Chief Risk Officer

GRC Technology Legal Advisor

Combining legal expertise with technological solutions for GRC. This emerging path is ideal for lawyers with a strong interest in technology. Responsibilities might include:

- Advising on the implementation of GRC software solutions
- Developing legal and compliance content for GRC platforms
- Ensuring GRC technologies align with legal and regulatory requirements
- Bridging the gap between legal, compliance, and IT teams

Possible Career Progression: GRC Analyst → GRC Technology Specialist → GRC Technology Legal Advisor

Regulatory Affairs Specialist

Focusing on navigating regulations, often in highly regulated industries like healthcare or financial services. This role involves:

- Monitoring and interpreting regulatory changes
- Developing strategies for regulatory compliance
- Liaising with regulatory bodies
- Advising on the impact of regulations on business operations

Possible Career Progression: Regulatory Affairs Associate → Regulatory Affairs Manager → Head of Regulatory Affairs

Ethics and Integrity Officer

Developing and maintaining ethical standards within an organization. This role focuses on:

- Creating and implementing codes of conduct
- Developing ethics training programs

- Managing ethics hotlines and investigations
- Advising on ethical decision-making

Possible Career Progression: Ethics Analyst → Ethics Manager → Chief Ethics Officer

Focus on SMEs

For lawyers interested in GRC careers focused on SMEs, there are unique opportunities and skill sets to develop:

- Become a generalist with broad knowledge across various GRC areas.
- Develop strong business acumen to understand the operational realities of SMEs.
- Hone project management skills to implement GRC initiatives with limited resources.
- Gain expertise in scalable GRC technologies suitable for smaller organizations.
- Build a network within SME-focused business associations and chambers of commerce.

Career paths might include becoming an outsourced GRC advisor for multiple SMEs, specializing in GRC consulting for high-growth start-ups, or working with SME-focused legal tech companies. The key is to position oneself as a pragmatic problem solver who can translate GRC requirements into actionable, affordable solutions for smaller businesses.

Government Roles in GRC

The public sector offers numerous opportunities for lawyers to specialize in GRC-related areas:

Regulatory Agency Counsel

Working within government agencies to develop, interpret, and enforce regulations. For example, this could be in agencies such as the Securities and Exchange Commission (SEC), Environmental Protection Agency (EPA), or Food and Drug Administration (FDA).

Possible Career Progression: Staff Attorney → Senior Attorney → Assistant General Counsel → General Counsel

Legislative Counsel

Drafting and reviewing legislation related to governance, risk, and compliance matters. This role involves working with lawmakers to shape GRC-related requirements.

Possible Career Progression: Legislative Aide → Legislative Analyst → Senior Legislative Counsel

Government Inspector General

Overseeing compliance and integrity within government agencies. This role involves conducting audits, investigations, and evaluations to ensure government operations are efficient, effective, and free from fraud, waste, and abuse.

Possible Career Progression: Inspector → Senior Inspector → Deputy Inspector General → Inspector General

Enforcement Attorney

Working in the enforcement divisions of regulatory agencies to investigate and prosecute violations of laws and regulations.

Possible Career Progression: Enforcement Attorney → Senior Enforcement Attorney → Assistant Director of Enforcement → Director of Enforcement

International Roles for Lawyers in GRC

The globalization of business has created a wealth of international opportunities for lawyers in GRC across various sectors. In-house counsel at multinational corporations often find themselves at the forefront of international GRC efforts, developing and implementing global compliance programs, managing cross-border risks, and ensuring adherence to diverse regulatory requirements across multiple jurisdictions. These roles may include titles such as global compliance officer, international legal counsel, or head of international regulatory affairs. In-house lawyers might be based at global headquarters, coordinating worldwide GRC efforts, or in regional hubs, managing GRC for specific geographical areas.

Government lawyers also play a range of roles in international GRC, working for regulatory bodies or international organizations or in diplomatic roles. They may be involved in developing international standards, negotiating cross-border agreements, or facilitating regulatory cooperation between nations. In law firms and consulting firms, lawyers can specialize in international GRC, advising clients on global compliance strategies, conducting cross-border investigations, or helping organizations navigate international regulatory landscapes. These roles might include positions such as international compliance consultant, global risk advisory partner, or Foreign Corrupt Practices Act (FCPA) specialist. Some lawyers may also find opportunities with nongovernmental organizations (NGOs) or international bodies like the United Nations, working on global governance issues, anti-corruption efforts, or international development projects with a GRC focus. Regardless of the sector, these international roles offer lawyers the chance to operate on a global stage, tackling multi-jurisdictional GRC challenges and contributing to the development of global best practices in governance, risk management, and compliance.

Lawyers in law firms play a particularly significant role in international GRC, often serving as external experts and advisors to both multinational corporations and smaller companies expanding globally. These roles can be highly specialized and offer opportunities for lawyers to develop deep expertise in specific areas of international GRC:

- **International Compliance and Investigations:** Law firm lawyers often lead cross-border internal investigations, helping clients uncover and address potential violations of anti-corruption laws, sanctions, or other international regulations. They may work on high-profile Foreign Corrupt Practices Act (FCPA) cases or assist with compliance with the UK Bribery Act across multiple jurisdictions.
- **Global Risk Advisory:** Many large law firms have dedicated global risk advisory practices in which lawyers help clients identify,

assess, and mitigate risks associated with international operations. This might involve conducting due diligence on foreign business partners, advising on the risk implications of entering new markets, or developing global risk management frameworks.

- **International Regulatory Compliance:** As regulations become increasingly globalized, law firm lawyers often specialize in helping clients navigate specific regulatory regimes across multiple countries. This could include advising on global data protection laws, international financial regulations, or cross-border environmental compliance.
- **Trade and Sanctions Compliance:** With the expansion of international trade laws and sanctions regimes, many law firm lawyers specialize in this area, helping clients ensure compliance with export controls, economic sanctions, and trade regulations across different jurisdictions.
- **Cross-Border M&A and Transactions:** Lawyers working on international deals help ensure that GRC aspects are properly addressed. This includes conducting compliance due diligence, structuring deals to mitigate international regulatory risks, and advising on post-merger integration of GRC programs.
- **International Dispute Resolution:** When GRC issues lead to cross-border disputes, law firm lawyers with expertise in international arbitration and litigation represent clients and navigate jurisdictional issues.

Lawyers in these roles often have the opportunity to work on high-stakes matters that span multiple countries and legal systems. They may be based in their home country but travel frequently, or they might work from international offices of global law firms. The ability to coordinate with local counsel in different jurisdictions, manage multijurisdictional teams, and synthesize legal requirements into practical advice for clients is highly valued. These positions often require a combination of technical legal expertise, business acumen, project management skills, and cultural sensitivity.

Moreover, as the demand for international GRC expertise grows, some law firms are developing innovative service models, such as setting up separate GRC consulting arms or partnering with other professional services firms to offer integrated GRC solutions. This trend is creating new and evolving opportunities for lawyers to apply their skills in multidisciplinary global contexts.

Key Skills to Develop

Success in GRC requires a combination of legal expertise, business acumen, and specialized GRC skills. Key areas for development include:

Legal Skills

- Regulatory interpretation and application
- Contract drafting and analysis
- Legal risk assessment
- Policy development
- Litigation management (for enforcement roles)
- Legislative drafting (for government roles)

Business Skills

- Strategic thinking and business acumen
- Project management
- Data analysis and interpretation
- Technology proficiency
- Communication and presentation skills
- Change management
- Leadership and team collaboration
- Stakeholder management
- Negotiation skills

Technical GRC Skills

- Risk assessment and management
- Compliance program development and implementation
- Corporate governance best practices
- Audit planning and execution
- Ethical decision-making frameworks
- Investigation techniques
- Crisis management

Education and Certifications

As the field of governance, risk, and compliance (GRC) continues to evolve and become more complex, lawyers working in this area need ongoing professional development. Specialized certifications can provide valuable knowledge, credibility, and recognition of expertise in various aspects of GRC. This section explores key certifications that are particularly relevant for lawyers in GRC roles.

OCEG Certifications

OCEG offers a range of highly relevant certifications for GRC professionals, including lawyers. These certifications are particularly attractive due to their comprehensive coverage of GRC topics and their accessibility through the OCEG All-Access Pass. OCEG offers a full certification suite with no additional fees beyond the All-Access Pass. The certifications in the suite integrate with each other and offer a full GRC education.

1. **GRC Professional (GRCP) Certification:** This certification is recommended for all lawyers involved in any GRC role or with ongoing GRC tasks. It provides a solid foundation in GRC principles and practices.
2. **GRC Auditor (GRCA):** Certification is highly recommended for lawyers involved in driving or supporting assessments and assurance regarding GRC capabilities.
3. **Integrated Audit and Assurance Professional (IAAP) Certification:** Lawyers who want to delve deeper into assurance and audit techniques should consider this certification. It provides advanced knowledge in audit and assurance practices.
4. **Integrated Policy Management Professional (IPMP) Certification:** This certification offers specialized knowledge in creating, implementing, and managing effective policies and the overall policy management capability.
5. **Integrated Compliance and Ethics Professional (ICEP) Certification:** This is recommended for lawyers in any GRC role as compliance relies heavily on their involvement.
6. **Integrated Risk Management Professional (IRMP) Certification:** This is a useful certification for any lawyer engaged, even minimally,

in directly providing support and guidance to those with primary responsibility for risk management.

7. **Integrated Data Privacy Professional (IDPP) Certification:** Lawyers engaged in ensuring data privacy compliance should consider this certification. It provides comprehensive knowledge of data privacy principles and practices within the broader GRC context.
8. **Integrated AI Professional (IAIP) Certification:** This is an extremely timely and important certification, offering lawyers a starting education in the ways AI must be governed and its risks and compliance requirements controlled.
9. **Additional Certifications:** At the time of this book's publication, OCEG is developing additional certifications of value to lawyers, including the Integrated Governance and Oversight Professional (IGOP) and Integrated Strategy and Performance Professional (ISPP).

OCEG certifications offer several unique advantages:

1. **Cost-Effectiveness:** All OCEG certifications, including self-directed prep courses, exams, and continuing education, are included at no additional cost for OCEG All-Access Pass holders.
2. **Flexibility:** Preparation courses and exams are available on demand online, allowing professionals to learn and certify at their own pace.
3. **Integrated Approach:** OCEG certifications take an integrated view of GRC, which aligns well with lawyers' evolving role in this field.
4. **Continuous Learning:** The continuing education provided by OCEG ensures that certified professionals stay up to date with the latest developments in GRC.

Other Relevant Certifications

In addition to OCEG certifications, there are other certifications that lawyers in GRC roles might consider, including:

- **Certified Internal Auditor (CIA):** Offered by the Institute of Internal Auditors (IIA). For lawyers deeply involved in audit functions, this globally recognized certification provides a solid foundation in internal auditing.

- **Certified Information Privacy Professional (CIPP):** Offered by the International Association of Privacy Professionals (IAPP). This certification is valuable for lawyers focusing on data privacy and protection, offering in-depth knowledge of privacy laws and regulations. It is a good companion to OCEG's IDPP certification, which more directly addresses the integrated GRC needs in privacy management.
- **Certified in Risk and Information Systems Control (CRISC):** Offered by ISACA. This certification can be valuable for lawyers involved in IT risk management and information systems control.
- **Certified Compliance and Ethics Professional (CCEP):** Offered by the Society of Corporate Compliance and Ethics (SCCE). This is a useful certification for lawyers fully in compliance roles and is a good companion to OCEG's ICEP certification.
- **Certified Government Auditing Professional (CGAP):** Offered by the Institute of Internal Auditors. This is useful for lawyers engaging in audit of governmental processes.
- **Certified Fraud Examiner (CFE):** Offered by the Association of Certified Fraud Examiners. This is useful for lawyers focused on fraud investigations and audits.

Choosing the Right Certification

When selecting a certification, lawyers should consider:

1. Their current role and responsibilities in GRC
2. Future career aspirations in the GRC field
3. The specific needs and focus areas of their client organizations
4. Time and resources available for study and examination preparation
5. How certifications may build on each other

For lawyers working in GRC roles, pursuing relevant certifications can provide numerous benefits. These include enhancing knowledge and skills, gaining recognition for expertise, and staying current with best practices in the field. The OCEG certifications, in particular, offer a comprehensive and accessible path to professional development in GRC.

As the GRC landscape continues to evolve, lawyers require ongoing learning and professional development to maintain their effectiveness and advance their careers in this field. By carefully selecting and pursuing appropriate certifications, you can position yourself as a valuable asset in navigating the world of governance, risk, and compliance.

Networking and Professional Development

Building a strong professional network can help build a successful GRC career. Consider these strategies:

Join Professional Associations and GRC Organizations

- OCEG
- Association of Corporate Counsel (ACC)
- Society of Corporate Compliance and Ethics (SCCE)
- Institute of Internal Auditors (IIA)
- Information Systems Audit and Control Association (ISACA)
- The American Bar Association (ABA) business law section and sections addressing specific regulatory compliance subjects

Attend Conferences and Seminars

- Local GRC organizations' conferences
- Relevant ABA section events
- GRC technology and advisory firm events
- Industry-specific conferences

Participate in Online Forums and Discussion Groups

- LinkedIn groups focused on GRC, compliance, or risk management
- Legal forums like Lexology or JD Supra
- Government-focused platforms like GovLoop for public sector roles

Seek Mentorship

- Connect with experienced GRC professionals on LinkedIn and directly.

- Participate in mentorship programs in your organization or professional associations.
- Seek out mentorship opportunities to learn about emerging trends and technologies.

Contribute to the Field

- Author articles for legal or GRC publications.
- Speak at industry events or webinars.
- Participate in or lead professional association committees.
- Contribute to OCEG open-source GRC frameworks or standards projects.

Continuous Learning

- Stay updated on regulatory changes through legal research platforms.
- Follow GRC thought leaders on social media.
- Subscribe to relevant journals and newsletters.
- Participate in webinars and online courses from OCEG, the ABA, and others.

Career Advancement Strategies

To advance your GRC career, consider these strategies:

- **Develop a Specialization:** Focus on a specific area of GRC, such as AI governance, data privacy, financial compliance, or environmental regulations, to become a sought-after expert.
- **Gain Cross-Functional Experience:** To broaden your expertise, seek opportunities to work on projects that span various aspects of GRC. In government roles, look for inter-agency projects or task forces.
- **Stay Current with Technology:** Familiarize yourself with GRC technologies and how they are reshaping the field. For government roles, understand how technology is transforming public sector operations and compliance.
- **Pursue Leadership Roles:** To develop your management skills, look for opportunities to lead GRC initiatives or teams. In government, seek out roles on special committees or in working groups.

- **Participate in Continuous Learning:** Stay updated on regulatory changes, emerging risks, and evolving best practices in GRC. For government roles, pay attention to policy trends and legislative developments.
- **Build a Personal Brand:** Establish yourself as a thought leader through writing, speaking engagements, and active participation in professional associations.
- **Consider Rotation Programs:** If available, participate in rotation programs that allow you to experience several aspects of GRC or different government agencies.
- **Pursue Advanced Degrees:** Consider an LLM in a relevant field, an MBA, or a specialized master's degree in areas like risk management or public administration for government roles.
- **Leverage Public-Private Sector Transitions:** Experience in both sectors can be highly valuable. Consider how you might transition between public and private sector roles to broaden your expertise.

Conclusion

Building a successful career in GRC offers you a unique opportunity to combine legal expertise with strategic business acumen, technological savvy, and ethical leadership. Whether in the private sector or government, the field presents diverse pathways for professional growth and impact.

By focusing on skill development, building a strong professional network, pursuing relevant certifications, and staying current with industry trends, you can position yourself as a valuable asset in the ever-evolving world of GRC. Remember, a career in GRC is not just about compliance—it is about driving organizational integrity, managing risks effectively, and contributing to sustainable success in both business and governance.

As you progress in your GRC career, you have the opportunity to shape the way organizations and government entities approach governance, manage risks, and ensure compliance. Your expertise is instrumental in building trust, promoting transparency, and fostering ethical practices that benefit not just individual organizations but society as a whole.

The journey may be challenging, but a career in GRC can be immensely rewarding and impactful for those who embrace it.

Action Items

- Conduct a self-assessment of your GRC skills and knowledge, identifying areas for professional development.
- Create a personal development plan that includes specific GRC-related goals, such as obtaining relevant certifications.
- Identify mentorship and networking opportunities within your organization or industry to further your GRC expertise.
- Develop a strategy for building your personal brand as a GRC expert, such as writing articles or speaking at conferences.
- Create a plan for cross-functional experience, identifying opportunities to work on GRC projects outside your typical legal role.

Index

actions, controls and, 59–61
AI. *See* artificial intelligence (AI)
algorithmic bias, 92
alignment, 107
artificial intelligence (AI), 124–125, 128, 162–163
audit
  internal, 22
  resource, 146

bias, algorithmic, 92
blockchain, 125–127, 128, 163
board, as stakeholders, 108
business continuity, in crisis management, 117–118
business objectives, legal considerations *vs.*, 14–18
business plan, 49–58
business strategy, 14

capability improvement, 74–80
career, 173–186
CCEP. *See* Certified Compliance and Ethics Professional (CCEP)
certifications, for lawyers, 181–185
Certified Compliance and Ethics Professional (CCEP), 183
Certified Fraud Examiner (CFE), 183
Certified Government Auditing Professional (CGAP), 183
Certified Information Privacy Professional (CIPP), 183
Certified in Risk and Information Systems Control (CRISC), 183
Certified Internal Auditor (CIA), 182
CFE. *See* Certified Fraud Examiner (CFE)
CGAP. *See* Certified Government Auditing Professional (CGAP)
change identification, 78–80
change implementation, 78–80
change management, 30, 143
chief compliance officer, 174
chief risk officer, 174–175
CIA. *See* Certified Internal Auditor (CIA)
CIPP. *See* Certified Information Privacy Professional (CIPP)
clients, 3–4
climate change, 164
collaboration: compliance and, 22; cross-functional, 21–26; future trends in, 25; imperative of, 22; integration and, 19–20; lawyer as leader in, 25–26; leading, 24; measuring success in, 24; overcoming challenges in, 23–24; structures and processes in, 23
communication: effective, 16; of legal risks by lawyers, 148–152; reporting and, 62–64
compliance: approaches, 54–56, 57; artificial intelligence in, 128; collaboration and, 22;

cross-border, 45; monitoring, 127; proactive, 19; tracking, with blockchain, 125
confidentiality, 89–90, 151. *See also* data privacy
conflicts of interest, 91
context: external, 39–40; internal, 41–43; operational, 39–49; risk, 149
continuity of business, 117–118
continuous improvement, 2, 17, 107, 152–154
contracts, smart, 126
controls: actions and, 59–61; in regulation, 29–30
credibility, 107, 152
CRISC. *See* Certified in Risk and Information Systems Control (CRISC)
crisis management: business continuity in, 117–118; defined, 115–116; ethical considerations in, 119; landscape, 115–116; learning after, 118–119; legal considerations in, 117; in risk management, 28; role of lawyers in, 115–120
cross-border ethical considerations, 92–93
cross-border integration, 32–34
C-suite, as stakeholders, 108
cultural competence, 33
cultural due diligence, 97
culture: embedded, 2; ethical, 93–94; organizational, 43–45; technology and, 130
cybersecurity, 22

data analytics, 127–129
data localization, 133
data mapping, 132
data minimization, 132
data privacy, 6, 30, 65, 125, 128, 131–132, 134, 163, 164
data sovereignty, 130, 132
decision-making: ethical, 93–94; lawyers in, 147; risk-informed, 15
distributed ledger technology, 125–127
Dodd-Frank Act, 68
due diligence, cultural, 97

education: lawyer, 181–185; training and, 64–66
emotional intelligence, 144, 151–152
empathy, 151
employees, as stakeholders, 108–109
environmental responsibility, 95
ethical balance, 97
ethical business context, 95–98
ethical culture, 93–94
ethical decision-making, 93–94
ethical differences, 97–98
ethical dilemmas, in international contexts, 96–97
ethical imperialism, 95
ethical landscape, 88–93
ethical leadership, 17
ethical obligations, 90–91
ethical relativism, 95
ethical standards, 95–96
ethical technology use, 92
ethics: with artificial intelligence, 162–163; in crisis management, 119
ethics and integrity officer, 175–176
events: discovery of favorable and unfavorable, 69–71; responding to, 71–73
executives, as stakeholders, 108

FCPA. *See* Foreign Corrupt Practices Act (FCPA)
Foreign Corrupt Practices Act (FCPA), 32, 45
Fox, Tom, 121–122

GDPR. *See* General Data Protection Regulation (GDPR)
General Data Protection Regulation (GDPR), 32, 126, 132
global-local balance, 33
goals, regulation and, 30–31
governance, risk management, and compliance (GRC): as driver of success, 1–4; -focused career building, 173–186; as framework, 2; future trends in, 161–167; government roles in, 176–177; landscape, 18; legal expertise in, integration of, 13–35; legal strategy and objectives of, 18–21; regulation and, 28–32
governance support, 19
GRC. *See* governance, risk management, and compliance (GRC)
GRC Capability Model, 1, 37, 38
GRC Glossary, 1

Hill, Bettye, 111–114
human resources, 22

identity management, 126
incentivization, of conduct, 66–67
innovation, compliant, 15–16
integration, 2; collaborative, 19–20; cross-border, of legal expertise, 32–34
international roles, for lawyers, 177–180
Internet of Things (IoT), 129
IoT. *See* Internet of Things (IoT)
issue notification, 68–69

key compliance indicators (KCIs), 76
key performance indicators (KPIs), 20, 76
key risk indicators (KRIs), 28, 76

lawyers: as advisors, 138–141; as business partners, 138–141; career building for, GRC-focused, 173–186; certifications for, 181–185; communication of legal risk by, 148–152; in continuous improvement, 152–154; core role of, 39–56; corporate, 6–8; in crisis management, 115–120; dual roles of, 138–141; education for, 181–185; elevation of role of, 21; emotional intelligence of, 144; evolving role of, 165–166; government roles for, 176–177; international roles for, 177–180; as leaders, 21–26; networking for, 184–185; overreliance on experience and intuition by, 142; professional development for, 184–185; as protectors, 4–5; public sector, 8–9; resource constraints and, 144–148; skills for, 180; in stakeholder management, 105–110; in strategic prioritization, 145–146; strengths of, 141–142
leadership: in collaboration, lawyers in, 25–26; collaboration practices and, 24; cross-functional collaboration and, 21–26; ethical, 17; executive, 23; role of, 148
legal strategy: GRC objectives and, 18–21; integrated, 19
legal touchpoints, 18–19

machine learning (ML), 124–125, 162–163
media, as stakeholders, 109
Mitchell, Scott, 167–171
ML. *See* machine learning (ML)
Murphy, Joe, 99–103

natural language processing (NLP), 127

nepotism, 95
networking, for lawyers, 184–185
NLP. *See* natural language processing (NLP)

objective-setting criteria, 52–53, 56–57
obligation identification, 53–54, 57
obstacle identification, 53–54, 57
OCEG, 1, 4–5, 36, 37, 181–182
Open Compliance & Ethics Group (OCEG), formerly, ix, 1
operating effectiveness, 75–77
operating efficiency, 75–77
operational context, 39–49
operationalization, of GRC strategies, 59–73
opportunity identification, 53–54, 57
organizational culture, 43–45

Paik, Son-U Michael, 35–38
performance metrics, 20
policy creation and management, 61–62
predictive analytics, 127
Principled Performance, 1n1, 7
proactive management, 107
process automation, robotic, 129
process mining, 127
process standardization, 33
professional development, 184–185
protectors, lawyers as, 4–5
public, as stakeholders, 109

regulation: change management and, 30; climate change and, 164; critical controls in, 29–30; goals an, 30–31; high, navigating GRC in, 28–32; intensive oversight in, 29; international landscapes and, 45; shifting landscape of, 163–164
regulatory affairs specialist, 175
reporting: automated regulatory, 128; communication and, 62–64
resource allocation, 107
resource audit, 146
resource constraints, 144–148
resource management, 146–147
reward approaches, 54–56, 57
risk approaches, 54–56, 57
risk assessment, 26–27, 33, 142
risk-based approach, 19
risk communication, 148–152
risk contextualization, 149
risk identification, 26
risk-informed decision-making, 15
risk management, 22, 155; legal role in, 26–28
risk mitigation, 27
risk monitoring, 27–28
risk narratives, 150
risk quantification, 16–17
robotic process automation (RPA), 129
RPA. *See* robotic process automation (RPA)

Sarbanes-Oxley Act, 68
sentiment analysis, 128
Seymour, Judit, 82–85
small and medium enterprises (SMEs), 50, 124, 158, 159, 161, 176
SMEs. *See* small and medium enterprises (SMEs)
stakeholder capitalism, 165
stakeholder management: challenges in, 110; GRC capabilities and, 107; role of lawyers in, 105–110; strategies, 108–109
stakeholders, 22–23, 46–48
Strassberg, Jonathan, 157–160
strategic alignment, 2
strategic enablement, 19
strategic prioritization, 145–146
supply chain traceability, 126

technology: adoption, 2, 134–135; artificial intelligence, 124–125, 128, 162–163; blockchain, 125–127, 128, 163; challenges, 133–134; competence, 134; culture and, 130; data analytics, 127–129; economic factors and, 130; ethical use of, 92; future of, 124–129; implementation, 131; infrastructure, 130; international adoption of, factors in, 129–130; landscape, 123–124; legal advisor, 175; leveraging, 33; machine learning, 124–125; overreliance on, 92, 134; proficiency, 143; road map, 134; trends in, 129; use, 123–135; visualization, 127–129
training, education and, 64–66
transparency, 89–90
trust, 94

value, 18
visualization technology, 127–129

whistleblowing, 90–91